READING
FOR MEANING
IN THE
ELEMENTARY SCHOOL

READING
FOR MEANING
IN THE
ELEMENTARY SCHOOL

RICHARD L. HENDERSON
Emory University

DONALD ROSS GREEN
California Test Bureau

PRENTICE-HALL, INC., *Englewood Cliffs, New Jersey*

Library of Congress Catalog Card Number 70-76305
Printed in the United States of America
Current printing (last digit):
10 9 8 7 6 5 4 3 2 1

Prentice-Hall International, Inc., *London*
Prentice-Hall of Canada, Ltd., *Toronto*
Prentice-Hall of Australia, Pty. Ltd., *Sydney*
Prentice-Hall of India Private Ltd., *New Delhi*
Prentice-Hall of Japan, Inc., *Tokyo*

To Kay and Mary

FOREWORD

My flight late last night from Chicago to Los Angeles was unusually pleasant and rewarding. I read the little book you are about to read. Fortunately I had just come from a conversation about the teaching of reading, and so I was unusually receptive to what the book is about. My "set," as the authors term one's state of readiness, was positive.

Mortimer Adler and I had been agreeing, a few hours earlier, that teaching a child basic skills, such as word recognition, is merely the primitive beginning in the reading process. The real business of reading, as Professors Henderson and Green make clear (crystal clear!), is bringing meaning to and drawing meaning from the printed page. What individuals derive from even great literary works depends in large measure on what they bring to them, and is related to fundamental reading skills in about the same instrumental way that the ability to drive nails is related to the construction of an aesthetically satisfying house.

The book is deceptively simple in message and structure. The central theme appears again and again in many contexts. This is not a book on methods and techniques for the teaching of reading. The authors do not participate in the apparently endless and rather unproductive debate over which among several methods is most effective. If Rip Van Winkle had gone to sleep in the midst of it twenty years ago, he might well wake up today, identify quickly with familiar rhetoric, and say, "Ho hum!" Professors Henderson and Green do not take lightly the issues involved and have conducted significant research relevant to them. But they address themselves to another matter—that of lifetime encounters with the written word and how to make them more meaningful and romantic. Rightly, I think, they suggest that their book is likely to be most salient for teachers of the upper elementary school years.

After a brief prologue the authors set forth, in an entire chapter, their definition of reading. They involve the reader—make him work—and thus put into practice one of their basic teaching principles. Then they introduce him to the varied character of meanings in a fascinating chapter that left me somewhat frustrated but that aroused my curiosity and a desire to probe deeper into some of those tantalizing references at the end of the chapter. I hope you will; this was the authors' intent.

Next I was introduced to the study of language and thought of Alice and her discovery that she had been speaking prose all her life. In Chapter V, I began to wonder what propositions regarding the nature of learning have to do with reading for meaning. But then it all became clear in the next chapter. In a series of skillfully presented and analyzed teaching episodes the authors put it all together: meaning, language, learning, and the sensitive relating of all three.

Clearly, from my observations of elementary education, what Professors Henderson and Green are talking about does not now significantly guide teaching and learning, especially in the upper elementary school years. We undertake very little instruction in the fundamentals of reading after the lower elementary years, but children need to read more and more. They are expected to bring meaning to and derive meaning from printed materials variously estimated as being from four to six times more complex conceptually than the printed matter prepared specifically for teaching them to read.

Teachers at all levels need to understand what is involved in reading for meaning and to develop, subsequently, appropriate techniques. The present book is devoted primarily to the first of these concerns but, comprehended, has significant implications for the second.

Perhaps you will bring more meaning to succeeding pages if you know something about the authors. Professor Henderson began his career as a teacher of high school English. His interest in language, and particularly in the reading process, led him into the field of elementary education, where he has worked as a teacher, administrator, and college instructor for many years. Professor Green began as a teacher of high school mathematics, which led to an interest in learning and cognitive development. His research on learning and instruction, and the problems raised by the students in his classes in educational psychology, led him to focus his attention on intellectual growth in the elementary school and perforce on reading.

This is not just another "ivory tower" imposition upon the unsuspecting (or perhaps suspicious) teacher. The authors practice what they preach, as hundreds of their students can testify. Read this book, then, and teach for meaning.

JOHN I. GOODLAD

John I. Goodlad is Dean, Graduate School of Education, University of California, Los Angeles, and Director, Research and Development Division, Institute for Development of Educational Activities, Incorporated.

PREFACE

This book is designed to help you—teachers and teachers-to-be, as well as interested parents—understand the fundamental nature of the reading act.

It was written out of the conviction that if one is to design effective methods and techniques of teaching reading or to judge their value, he must first understand the nature of the process he is dealing with. Hence, we offer this "pre-methods" book as an introduction—or at least as a companion book—to the study of methodology.

We hope it will be evident that what we have to say is relevant to reading instruction at all stages of learning. We do care about initial instruction, but the material of this book may well prove most helpful to those teaching beyond grade one, since we find that first-grade teachers are usually more careful about what they do in reading instruction than are teachers on up the line.

Our approach is first to describe what we know about the reading process—what people do when they learn to read. Then, since reading may be described as learning how to get meanings from language in print, we go on in succeeding chapters to analyze *meaning, language,* and *learning* in order to make clear their roles in the process. Finally, we present a number of classroom vignettes that illustrate how these factors interact as teachers guide children's reading experiences.

You will note that much of the paraphernalia of standard texts is missing from this book. There are no exercises, lists of questions to be considered, no instructor's manual (i.e., no set of prepared test items), and no suggested readings. We do provide a list of references at the end of each chapter, most of which are worth perusal, but we know that if you have taken the trouble to look at the field of reading at all you are already overwhelmed with suggested and possible readings. In any case, we have planned this as a book to be read (see Chapter II) in contrast to a book to be studied (that is, pored over, chewed to pieces, and disgorged for a test).

We would like to acknowledge here our debt to Professor Fred Smith of the University of Oregon and to Dr. George Flamer of the California Test Bureau for their help with our discussion of language.

R. L. H.
D. R. G.

CONTENTS

READING
FOR MEANING
IN THE
ELEMENTARY SCHOOL

CHAPTER I

PROLOGUE

*This is an instance of the general truth, that
our progress in clarity of knowledge is primarily from the composition to its ingredients
(8, p. 213).*

Probably no school subject in history has received more attention from
educators, and from laymen as well, than reading. It has been, and doubtless will continue to be, the most important of the three R's. Highly complex democratic societies such as ours depend for their very existence on
a rational and literate citizenry. Hence they demand of their people an
extensive formal educational preparation, the chief aim of which is the
development of adequate reading skills. In such societies and under such
circumstances, the first R is unlikely to yield its primary position. Indeed,
it is impossible to think of education without thinking of reading; school
is reading. W. W. Charters puts the matter thus—perhaps too strongly:

> A man can pick up enough arithmetic for ordinary purposes outside
> school. He learns to talk before he enters school. The pattern of his char-
> acter is set in his home. It does not matter greatly if he cannot write. His
> knowledge of health, history, literature and politics he can pick up for
> himself if he knows how to read. Strip the curriculum to its bare essentials,
> and the three R's do not remain. There is only this one supreme essential
> R—the ability to read with speed and comprehension (1, p. 70).

Teachers of children concern themselves mainly with the problems of
reading instruction. Parents judge their children's progress by their growth
in reading ability. Administrators gauge the standings of their schools by
their rankings on standardized reading tests. From time to time, critics
of the public schools single out reading instruction as the target for their
attacks. Publishers issue textbooks on the methodology of reading by the

hundreds of thousands and graded readers by the millions. Nor, as Frank Jennings points out, are the schools and publishers alone concerned:

> Today, American business spends more time, money, and energy on in-service education than we as a nation spend on our public and private schools. Major insurance companies find that it pays to give employees courses to improve their reading skills (4, p. 34).

Truly, the business of reading is one of vast significance and proportions, educationally as well as economically and sociologically. As a teacher, whether of younger or older children, your major concern will certainly be the guidance of pupils' reading activities. As your pupils succeed in developing reading competence, so will they possess the major tool for success in other areas of the school program.

Yet to be an effective guide of children's growth in reading, one must know a good deal more than the mechanics of reading and the various techniques and approaches to reading instruction. Techniques and approaches are important, to be sure, but they are effective only to the extent that they develop out of the nature of the process under consideration. Too often we forget what ought to be obvious: The *nature of the reading process* must determine how we go about helping people learn to read!

We have written this book, therefore, to try to make clear the essential nature of reading as the *process of securing meaning through language in print.* Unlike most, if not all, texts on the subject of reading, this is not a book of prescriptions, of "how-to-do-its." Rather, it is an approach to the problems of reading instruction developed around the reading process itself.

We are not suggesting that directions for helping children develop specific skills and understandings are of no value. What we do contend is that most treatments of the role of meaning in reading are usually too brief (or too superficial) to develop the basic and essential structure out of which specific techniques ought to arise. And this is to say that skill-development techniques, which logically should develop out of the nature of the reading process as getting meanings, are commonly presented as separate activities whose sum, somehow, should add up to the ability to read. To stretch a figure, methods too often tend to be limbs tacked on to the "body" of reading rather than growing naturally out of it. This is why the thesis of this book is that the "body" of reading is getting meaning from language in print. We believe that until this aspect of reading is understood, you cannot make intelligent use of the many techniques and procedures in reading instruction found in texts and manuals.

Note that there is another aspect of reading pointed out by Russell and Fea who state, "In essence, the reading act is divisible into two processes: (1) identifying the symbol, and (2) obtaining meaning from the recognized symbol" (6, p. 868). To the first process we are paying little direct attention, because it is only at the initial stages of reading that the teacher has to be concerned with symbol identification as a separate and distinct operation, and because consideration of this process does require attention to skill development and particular techniques. Thus to include it, would distract from our concern with the second process, reading as getting meaning.

Our task is not a simple one, however, for no one completely understands the business of getting meaning from printed language. To understand completely would be to know exactly what goes on inside human minds when they engage in the most complex intellectual task. For the present, at least, this knowledge is not at hand. We hope and expect that as time passes we will come closer to this goal. However, even though the last word has not been said, some things are known and are worth your attention.

We therefore propose in this book to spend considerable time spelling out what we like to call the three "basic ingredients" of the reading process: the ingredient of *meaning*, the ingredient of *language*, and the ingredient of *learning*. In succeeding chapters we shall present rather detailed discussions of each of these basic ingredients and, in conclusion, show how they all work together in the classroom.

You will observe that we do not talk about or describe specifically any of the several current approaches to reading instruction, whether conventional (as a basal reader approach) or otherwise (as, say, a programmed approach). We would particularly like to make it clear that in spite of our conviction about the centrality of meaning in the reading process, we do not believe this conviction or any others we hold dictate a position on what Chall has called "the great debate" (2). Thus we note that Chall reports that all of the methods she observed and surveyed have children read for meaning (2, p. 343) even though the "debate" is between "meaning-approaches" and "code emphasis" approaches.

We believe that almost all approaches have substantial merit in some circumstances and can be made to work adequately (i.e., most children can learn to read at least minimally well using any of these methods). The evidence used for comparing methods is almost entirely inadequate. Yet choices must be made. This book stems from the conviction that the more teachers understand the reading act the better the chances are that they will use *their choice* of method effectively.

Generally speaking, teachers need more freedom than they now have for pursuing reading instruction as they see fit rather than following prescriptions. Teachers have long been burdened with many don'ts, must nots, and prohibitions of all sorts. The "experts" often say "This can't be done," or "If you do that it will hurt the child." Few people realize just how thin is the evidence on which such assertions are based. For a discussion of why research has produced so little hard knowledge about the relative merits of the various methods, see Green (3, Ch. 5) or Wallen and Travers (7, Ch. 10) or Russell and Fea (6, pp. 875, 915).

Heavily researched though reading has been, the outstanding result is that practically everything anyone has tried has worked quite well in some classes with some teachers. Given a basic understanding of the reading process, you as a teacher can ignore admonitions and warnings and do the things that make sense to you in the situation you have at hand.

So, while we do refer to certain techniques on occasion, systematic discussions of particular approaches are omitted. Specific approaches are not at issue. What is at issue are the three basic ingredients of the reading process—meaning, language, and learning—which we are concentrating upon because they form the substructure of any and all approaches to reading instruction. As such, they take precedence over discussion of technique. As we have already suggested, these basic ingredients constitute the "body" of reading, out of which grow, or should grow, the particular techniques employed in instruction. In short, we are not dictating techniques; the approach is up to you. We do insist, however, that whatever approach you choose will be effective to the extent that you take account of what meaning, language, and learning have to offer in the way of both content and method.

We realize that the organization of most schools—the teacher-per-classroom plan—and the burden of nonteaching chores borne by teachers, make serious and sustained departures from traditional procedures difficult to arrange. It is easier, and often safer, to "operate within the system," to teach as others teach. We feel sure that as you follow us through these pages, you will often say, "Great idea—but who does it, and who'll let me try it?" On the other hand, accepting the likelihood of administrative, organizational, and assorted other restrictions on your activities, we are convinced that if you find what follows *meaningful,* you will find ways of implementing it.

Now a word of caution. This book cannot do the whole job. As a teacher of reading, you must continue to spend time with meaning, language, and learning. The more you know about the nature and development of meaning, about the nature and function of language, and about the nature of the learning process, the less dependent you will be on tricks, gimmicks, and mechanics as you teach. You will be able to take your cues for teaching from your materials and from your pupils. In consequence, your "methods" will not be arbitrary. They will have a natural relationship to the situation and will thus have a better chance of being effective.

There is more. To understand as fully as possible the nature of the reading process is imperative. Yet if you are to help children get at the marvelous variety of meanings available in their reading materials, you yourself must have a rich store. To be sure, we are here talking more about general education than we are about the specifics of reading instruction. But there is a reason. Ivor Richards provides it:

> There is no such thing as merely reading words; always through words we are trafficking, or trying to traffic, with things—things gone by, present, to come or eternal. So a person who sets up to teach reading should recognize that he may be more ambitious than he seems. He may pretend that he is only concerned to help people not to mistake one word for another, or one construction for another. That, so far, doesn't look like an attempt to finger the steering wheel of the universe. But "Which word is it?" turns into "Which use?"; and the question "Which construction?" into "What implication?" Before long, the would-be authority on interpretation has become indistinguishable from an authority on "What's what?"—a question which belongs to a more divine science than he may wittingly aspire to (5, p. 20).

Thus Richards warns us that teachers of reading are really "teachers of understanding," and that guiding reading experiences is clearly a matter of knowing a great deal about books and people and things and ideas and life. Children cannot simply be taught to read; they must be helped to learn as they read—to learn about the whole world: people, places, things, events. You can help them to learn through reading only if you have learned to read well, widely, and wisely:

> A good novel or a good book of travel will let you know more of the world than many a treatise: Only, for heaven's sake, think as you read. Try to imagine what it all means. Do not get a mere craving for print without thought. It is almost as bad as drink (8, p. 174).

Unfortunately, most students we know are kept so busy studying that they cannot take time to develop the habit of thinking as they read!

At any rate, Richards assures us that teachers assume a momentous responsibility, because they do have to "finger the steering wheel of the universe." They must therefore be at once humble and very wise. For teachers, above all others, a college education must not end on commencement day.

And so to reading.

Bibliography

1. Betts, Emmett A., *Foundations of Reading Instruction*. New York: American Book Company, 1954.
2. Chall, Jeanne, *Learning to Read: The Great Debate*. New York: McGraw-Hill Book Company, 1967.

3. Green, Donald Ross, *Educational Psychology*. Englewood Cliffs, N.J.: Prentice-Hall, Inc., 1964.

4. Jennings, Frank, "The New Dimension of Education," *Saturday Review*, Feb. 13, 1960. © 1960 Saturday Review, Inc.

5. Richards, I. A., *How to Read a Page*. New York: W. W. Norton & Company, Inc., 1942.

6. Russell, David H., and Henry R. Fea, "Research on Teaching Reading," in N. L. Gage, *Handbook of Research on Teaching*. Chicago: Rand McNally & Co., 1963.

7. Wallen, Norman E., and Robert M. W. Travers, "Analysis and Investigation of Teaching Method," in N. L. Gage, *Handbook of Research on Teaching*. Chicago: Rand McNally & Co., 1963.

8. Whitehead, Alfred North, *Essays in Science and Philosophy*. New York: Philosophical Library, 1947.

CHAPTER II

A LOOK
AT READING

We always read for some purpose—unless some
sad, mad, bad schoolteacher has got hold of us
(8, p. 20).

Let us begin our examination of the reading process with a device which
we think will help you get at the notion of reading far better than any
definition could, at least at the outset. Here are three passages, selected
from various sources. Please read them carefully and thoughtfully so that
we can discuss them.

1. $E = mc^2$
2. Nothing can possibly be conceived in the world, or even out of it,
   which can be called good without qualification, except a *good will*.
   Intelligence, wit, judgment, and the other talents of the mind, however
   they may be named . . . are undoubtedly good and desirable in many
   respects; but these gifts of nature may also become extremely bad and
   mischievous if the will which is to make use of them . . . is not good
   (5, p. 11).
3. One of the most recurring controversies in reading instruction is over
   whether or not today's children read as well, better, or worse than their
   counterparts of twenty, thirty, or forty years ago. Although such comparisons continue to be made, no really definitive answer is possible,
   since the instruments used to measure pupil progress in reading and
   pupil intelligence vary considerably from those of today (1, p. 1).

By taking the time to analyze the responses that we think you might
have made to these selections, we can better help you to understand the
nature of the reading process. In your responses lies the key to your notion
of reading language in print. Let's consider your reactions.

The first step you took was that of simply recognizing all of the words and other symbols. This you were able to do since each is a part of your "reading experience"—you have met them before, though in different contexts, and you remembered them as you encountered them in these passages. If you could not remember them, of course, you could not have gone on to the next step.

Your next step in reading the passages was that of "getting the drift" of each. That is, you developed some idea of what each is all about. You established some kind of setting, or frame of reference. You probably said to yourself something like this:

1. $E = mc^2$ is Einstein's key to atomic fission. Einstein was one of the greatest theoretical physicists of all time.

2. This writer is saying that good will is the only absolutely good thing in the world or out of it. He must be some kind of philosopher.

3. This writer is explaining why the reading achievement of today's children cannot be compared with the achievement of those of several decades ago.

So far, so good!

Now we may ask, how many of these passages did you *read?* You have identified the words and other symbols, and you have "gotten the drift." Therefore, you may say, you have read them all. Do not think us unduly severe, however, if we tell you that probably the only passage which you *read* was the last. Why? Let's explain why we think so.

SELECTION 1:   What does the equal sign mean in the formula? Are E and mc^2 the same things, or are m and c parts which combine to make E, or what? What units of measurement are involved? In what way is the formula related to actual events in the physical world? Did you *read* this equation? (Of course, *we* don't understand the concept or the language, either, which is why we assume that you do not! Only the competent physicist really *reads* this passage.)

SELECTION 2:   In this passage, the writer establishes human will as a faculty of the mind distinct from and superior to intelligence, wit, and judgment (among other talents). Do you agree that this is legitimate? Are wit, intelligence, and judgment really separate faculties of the mind? Could you argue sensibly with someone who believes they are not? Is the ability to argue this point necessary in order to understand this passage? Have you *read* this selection?

SELECTION 3:   In the third selection, the writer (you may have thought) points out that whether today's children read better than, as well as, or worse than yesterday's children is still a matter for dispute. However, since we measure reading achievement and intelligence differently today, we cannot settle the issue conclusively. Thus the *sense* of the paragraph is clear, even though you may not be familiar with techniques of measur-

ing reading achievement and intelligence. You do have the basic understanding that it is not reasonable to compare the effects of different school
programs unless you measure them with the same yardstick. You have
read this passage!

What can we conclude from all this? Since meaning does not reside in
the words and other symbols as such (even in the last passage), you had to
take acquired meanings to them in order, first, to recognize the words;
second, to get the drift; and finally, in the last passage, to fully understand. Perhaps you can now grasp more easily the notion of reading which
we may define as follows:

> Reading is the process of taking meaning *to,* in order to get meaning *from,*
> language in print.

Our illustrations have shown that recognizing words and getting the
drift, while necessary, were not sufficient to enable you to *read* (secure
the meanings of) the first two selections. All they did for you was simply to
put you "in a position" to read by giving you basic information (word
recognition) and a general orientation to the substance of the passages.
And when you were unable to take the appropriate meanings *to* the
substance, you could not move on to fuller understanding. You simply
remained "in a position" to read.

We are thus saying that reading goes considerably beyond these "first
steps," even though they are an important part of the process as we have
defined it. Reading does involve word recognition and getting the drift,
but beyond this, it involves the functioning of the "higher mental processes": reflecting, seeing relationships, solving problems, interpreting,
evaluating—in short, thinking, reasoning. Note that you exercised these
higher mental processes as you read the last passage. You reasoned that
is, you recognized through experience that the writer is correct in saying—
that comparing the "weights" of any two things requires the use of the
same scale. In other words, you went beyond recognizing words and getting
the drift; you took the next step into *reading-reasoning.* You took your
understanding of measurement in general *to* the passage and applied it to
get an understanding of the problem of comparing yesterday's children
with today's. So it is the notion of reading as reasoning, problem-solving,
or thinking, which we need very much to examine. It is the heart of the
process of reading.

From Word Recognition to Getting the Drift

Word recognition, the first step in the reading process, has often been
confused with word pronunciation. In the mid- and late-nineteenth century, for example, much, if not most, reading instruction was character-

ized by drills in "oral analysis." Children were drilled in phonics (sounds represented by letters, syllables, and words) from the outset of instruction. Day after day, and week after week, they struggled through *ab, eb, ib, ob, ub,* and *pam, pem, pim, pom, pum*. Great care was often taken to withhold meaningful materials until children's pronunciation skills were "perfected." And at least one authority held that if a child mastered word-sounds, meaning would take care of itself! Thus in 1889, Rebecca Pollard, in her *Synthetic Method,* assured the teacher that:

> If the instructions of the Manual are carefully followed (in inflection as well as in pronunciation), the child's own voice will give him a perfect understanding of what he reads (6, p. 11).

Pollard clearly assumed that word recognition automatically follows word pronunciation. Of course it often does, but not always and not automatically.

It seems clear that word sounds as such (except those of onomatopoetic words like *swish* and *bang*) have nothing whatever to do with meaning. You would have no trouble sounding out *phthisic, leucitohedron,* or *proteoclastic,* if we spelled them phonetically. But the sounds would not give you the slightest clues to meanings. This is not to say that we are unconcerned with phonology; for many reasons, including the need to recognize words, children should know how to "sound out" words. But it *is* to say that knowledge of sound does not invest words with meanings.

Turning to the fact that word recognition and getting the drift are the necessary but insufficient conditions for securing meaning, let us begin with word recognition. Suppose we write for you the word *table*. Since this word is, through your experience, practically a part of your nature, you recognize it at once. You then visualize some kind of table whose precise appearance depends on your experiences with tables. But does seeing the word suggest any further meaning? Can you tell what we had in mind when we wrote it for you? Clearly not; it is quite out of context. Hence, though you do take some meaning *to* the word, you cannot get meaning *from* it.

But now suppose we write, "We have a table which once belonged to Thomas Edison." The word now fits into a context; it relates to a whole range of tables in a unique way, and therefore takes on meanings. It is an antique, it was the property of a famous inventor and is therefore rare, and it must be valuable if in good condition. If you happen to be a collector of antiques, this table will hold a great many more meanings for you.

All of this is to say that information and ideas above the most elementary sort are not conveyed in print by single words; meanings are expressed by particular interrelationships between and among words, and unless the reader takes to passages an adequate understanding of the ideas, events, or situations to which the passages refer, these interrelationships cannot be grasped. The authors of *Language in General Education* make this dramatically clear by pointing out that by using only simple words chosen from the first 5,000 on the Thorndike list, one can prepare a composition totally beyond the comprehension of young readers, even though every word is "recognized" (7, pp. 59-60).

Thorndike made this point when, in 1917, he asked a number of sixth-grade children to interpret this sentence:

> In Franklin attendance upon school is required of every child between the ages of seven and fourteen on every day when school is in session unless the child is so ill as to be unable to go to school, or some person in his house is ill with a contagious disease, or the roads are impassable (10, p. 298).

Thorndike reported that ". . . the variety of the answers threatened to baffle all explanation. . . ." (10, p. 298).

Let us go on to observe what happens when children are required to explain a passage to which they cannot take the appropriate understandings. One group of fifth-grade children was asked to explain the following selection from their history book:

> Daniel Webster said of Alexander Hamilton, "He smote the rock of national resources and abundant streams of revenue burst forth. He touched the dead corpse of public credit and it sprang upon its feet."

After some thought, pupils produced the following absurdities:

> Daniel Webster said that Hamilton a plenty of government has burst forward. He put his hands on dead people and free to everybody and it grew to its feet. When he touched the dead they would spring to their feet.

> Daniel Webster said of Hamilton, "He stopped Mother Nature and fake rivers came instead. He stopped public credit and it was returned to him" (2).

These pupils showed by their written responses that they could identify many, if not all, of the words in the passage, and that they did try to "reason toward" meaning. Note, also, that despite knowing the words, they could not take the next step of getting the drift of the passage. The total context was simply beyond their experiences, hence beyond their comprehension. The words were not enough; their interrelationships provide the meaning, but the children could not fathom it because their experiences did not include situations relevant to that described in the passage. What experiences had pupils with revenue and public credit, to say nothing of figures of speech such as "the rock of national resources"?

In this connection, teachers who work with primary-level pupils tell us that the length and structure of words are not the major blocks to recognition and understanding. It is the objects or ideas to which the words refer that cause the trouble. Thus "intercontinental ballistic missile" may be more quickly recognized and understood than the little word "as."

You may recall that getting the drift of the equation and of the quotation from Kant did not enable you to move on to full understanding. Hence, getting the drift is essentially the orientation step—the necessary but insufficient step—that enables the reader to determine what a passage is all about. Having the setting, knowing the nature of the matter under consideration, the reader is in a position to call upon prior learnings related to the matter. He has developed an *orientation,* which gives direction and purpose to his attempts to create meanings.

> NOTE: We are here referring to what is commonly called *set,* a psychological term which you may have encountered in your studies. In our chapter on learning, we will deal at some length with the notion in order to make clear its role in learning and how it functions as one learns to read. For the present, we will simply leave you with a definition of *set* as a "temporary, but often recurrent, condition of the person . . . that (a) orients him . . . toward certain environmental stimuli or events rather than toward others, selectively sensitizing him . . . for apprehending them; (b) facilitates certain activities or responses rather than others" (3, p. 495).

Thus reading is a process which involves word recognition and getting the drift of passages. As we have emphasized, however, these are but the preliminaries. And they remain the preliminaries unless, by virtue of prior learnings, the higher mental processes enter in and enable us to produce meanings—to complete the *reading* process.

Reading As Getting Meanings

If a child sees and recognizes a word, he is, as we have noted, taking meaning *to* it. If he goes further and derives meaning *from* it, then he is *reading.* In order for this to happen, there must be some sort of context; that is, the word he recognizes must relate to something in the situation. This "something" is most often the other words in the sentence, paragraph, or book being read. But it can also be an object present or an event occurring at the time.

When single words are used as labels, they are in context and can be read. As an example, let us observe how school beginners might learn to read their first words. The teacher has printed on cards the symbols representing various pieces of furniture and has taped the cards to the appropriate objects: desk, chair, clock, and the like. Children can thus form an immediate association between the object (desk) and the symbol that represents it. They are learning.

But we must be clear at the outset that for a beginner this "association-forming" between written symbols and concepts—even as well-known a concept as *desk*—is not a simple process. Unlike a person who can already read, the beginner must put together a whole range of notions that are new to him, in whole or in part. He must call into play at that point his "higher mental processes" in order to understand that:

1. The combination of letters he sees represents the same idea that the spoken word does.
2. The combination of letters used represents the concept uniquely; no other combination serves just this purpose.
3. Whenever the symbol *desk* appears, the same concept is involved.
4. The particular desk present is only an example of the concept.
5. In this instance, the symbol is to be read as the label for this particular object.

Clearly, to learn all this is not a simple, single process!

Most children will need several repetitions of this situation in order to "fix" the association. Eventually, however, most will be able to *read* the word, even though the teacher disassociates it from the object by writing it on the chalkboard.

Adults, of course, have already learned such words. Even so, if upon entering the class, a parent saw the label *desk* affixed to a desk, he would probably either ignore it (not read it), or think something such as this: "The children are learning to read that word." Or perhaps, "Yes, that's a desk—big deal!" Without some such thinking process, we would have to conclude that, although the parent saw the word, he did not read it.

Here is a final illustration of the complicated reasoning process involved in reading even single words: Suppose while browsing in an antique shop, you come across an unknown and most curious object of metal and glass, vaguely resembling an old-fashioned water jug or carafe. The neck of the jug is sealed by a cork or plug, into which have been inserted two vertical tubes. One tube is a yard long and flexible; the other is short and terminates in what appears to be a metal pillbox. This strange object bears the label *Narghile.*

Since the label conjures up no notion of the use of the object, you cannot read it! So you set about a closer examination. The long tube, you note, ends in a kind of mouthpiece much like that of a modern cigarette holder. This suggests that the narghile may be some sort of smoking pipe. To test this hunch, you sniff the metal pillbox and discover the faint aroma of tobacco. Clearly this is a smoking pipe. But why the bowl-like base? Its shape, the presence of the plug, and the fact that it is hollow indicate that its function is to hold some kind of liquid. But why?

Further examination reveals that if one drew on the mouthpiece, any fumes produced in the pillbox would be sucked downward through the bowl on its passage to the mouth. Why this circuitous route? Obviously, to cause the fumes to pass through the liquid in the bowl. But to what purpose?

Two alternatives occur to you out of your experience: The liquid must either flavor the fumes, or heat or cool them. You eliminate the first possibility because you know (doesn't everyone?) that pipe tobacco is flavored by the process of steeping. You also eliminate the notion of heating the fumes, because the bowl is plainly too small to keep liquids hot for long. Thus you conclude that the narghile is an exotic water-cooled smoking pipe. You can now read the label *Narghile*.

Note how problem solving enters into the reading process. You actually had to play detective—call upon previous knowledge, put two and two together—in order to read the label. To be sure, you were dealing with a concrete object, whereas in print one deals with symbols; but the problem solving (thinking) process is as real in one as in the other.

> *Reading is the process of taking meaning to, in order to construct meaning from, language in print.*

Note that, faced with similar problems, we do not always move as slowly toward solutions as the length of this episode suggests. Thought can be as quick as lightning. In reality, this entire episode may have lasted but a few seconds. Moreover, habituated to certain kinds of writings and particular "families of ideas," we do not need *consciously* to probe for the relevant knowledge as we do when confronted by novel concepts or notions or problems to be solved. As we amass a greater and greater stock of concepts (established meanings), we need less and less to probe past experience (acquired knowledge) to derive meanings. For instance, you could read the last of our three passages quickly and easily because you understood the concepts and did not have to search memory for related knowledge. This was not true of Kant's statement—unless you are something of a philosopher!

Perhaps you can see from the examples we have given that even when dealing with single words, getting the drift (as well as recognizing words) is part of the thought processes of reading. But how this getting-the-drift step leads into the thinking required for getting the meaning is clearer when we deal with a passage containing many words. Remember the description we gave of getting the drift of the passage we acknowledged you *read*? We said:

> The writer is explaining why the reading achievement of today's children cannot be compared with the achievement of those of several decades ago.

This step led to, and made possible, the reasoning you used to derive meaning from the passage. Having understood this much, you were able to recall the notion that comparisons of performances need to be made in equivalent units if they are to be valid. Because you got the drift, your thinking was directed toward the *relevant* knowledge, and you were then prepared to apply it to get the writer's meaning. That is, you had the *set* needed to understand that "the issue cannot be settled conclusively because we measure reading achievement differently today from the way we did years ago."

Among the processes involved here, the act of recalling relevant knowledge and seeing how to use it to make sense of a paragraph or page is fundamental. It depends on getting the drift as well as on having the appropriate background knowledge. This application or use of prior knowledge, prior learning, is often called *transfer of training* by psychologists, who have long been impressed with the important role played by *set* in this central process.

Thus when you read the selection about reading and recognized that a reason for the difficulty in comparing achievements was being cited, you were led to think of a relevant aspect of your knowledge relating to measurement—that is, the requirement that comparisons presuppose measurement of the same kinds of things in the same units.

We acknowledge that you may well have gotten more meaning from the passage than we have given you credit for, but we insist that if you were unable to get this much, you were not *reading* the selection. There can be, and usually are, variations in the kinds and amounts of meaning people obtain from reading, but to be described as *reading*, they must derive some minimum amount of meaning from the material. Usually, the simplest way to demonstrate this minimum is to put the substance of the material into one's own words. For convenience, we will refer to this restatement of meaning as *translation*.

What *reasonings* beyond translation can be derived from our third selection? The range of possibilities is large, of course, but here are some that you may have thought of as you read:

1. We could use the old measures with today's children to make comparisons possible. The author overlooks this possibility.
2. However, to use the old measures would be inappropriate, because the unfamiliar formats and styles might be unfair to today's children; moreover, the objectives of instruction have changed so that the old tests don't measure the aspects we are concerned about now. For example, we no longer consider sheer speed in testing as important as the old tests did.
3. Comparisons with previous generations are silly anyway. Since the world changes so rapidly, such comparisons are really meaningless.

4. Even if we could make valid comparisons, we would not know why one group read (or reads) better than the other, which is really what we want to know. Furthermore, the relative merits of past and present instruction are not important. All that matters is, are we doing the best we can *now?*

5. People do argue about the strangest things!

Thus might you have reasoned beyond translation.

As we talk about the importance of going beyond translation—of reading beyond the minimum—you may feel the need for some term or label for this process. While it is possible, as other writers have demonstrated, to break up the "going-beyond" process into such functions as interpretation, interpolation, extrapolation, analysis, evaluation, and the like, the boundary lines between such functions are unclear at best. Therefore, we see no good reason to complicate matters by involving you in the task of identifying and sorting out these interrelated functions.

Do not think that we consider them unimportant, or that our discussions of the meanings to be derived from reading will be limited to translation. Quite the contrary. We hope, perhaps more than anything else, that you will come to appreciate the great value of extending to the fullest the meanings to be derived from reading, and that you will understand the ramifications and problems involved in doing so.

Children's Reading

So far, because for the most part we have been using you as the subject, we have not adequately described the reading process as it might go on in the classroom. We need now to turn to the school child himself and describe how he might go about reading materials presumed appropriate to his experience and ability. We shall begin with a passage from a story, "The Lost and Found Tree," in a "second level" basic reader:

> "Look at this black boot," said Dick. "It looks like a new one."
> Pete said, "It is a little boy's boot, but that boot is not Billy's."
> "I guess someone in our neighborhood lost it," said Dick.
> "I'll take the boot into the house. Maybe someone will come along and ask about it" (9, p. 7).

Most children, with or without help, will probably recognize the words in this story and will get the drift: This is a story about two boys finding a boot lost by a little boy in the neighborhood. Then they can move on to translate: Dick found a boot. Pete said it was a little boy's, but it wasn't Billy's. Dick said someone in the neighborhood lost it, so he would take it in the house in case somebody came for it.

The pupil who goes beyond translation, however, may reason somewhat as follows:

1. The boot is black and new. Are these facts important? Not so far.
2. How does Pete know the boot isn't Billy's? Why doesn't Dick know, too? They live in the same neighborhood and must know all the boys. Maybe Billy is Pete's brother.
3. Dick *guesses* that the boot belongs to someone in the neighborhood. What reason does he have for such a guess?

Here is a passage from a sixth-grade social studies text:

Galileo also discovered other laws of science through experiments. By dropping two balls of different sizes and different weights from the top of a tower in Pisa, Italy, and repeating this experiment several times, he proved that both balls fell at the same rate of speed. This proved that a Greek writer, Aristotle, had been wrong when he reasoned that a heavier object falls more rapidly than a lighter one. For centuries, people had thought Aristotle was right. Today Galileo is called the "first modern scientist" because he proved scientific laws through a series of experiments (4, p. 149).

Knowing the words, and getting the drift, the pupil may then go on to translate: Galileo dropped balls of different sizes and weights from a tower and proved that light and heavy objects fall at the same speed. He showed that Aristotle had been wrong about this for centuries. Galileo was called the "first modern scientist" because he proved ideas by experimenting. But again, the pupil going beyond translation might reason in one or more of the following ways:

1. Aristotle reasoned things out, but Galileo experimented. Experimenting is better than just reasoning things out, because this way you actually test things.
2. A good experiment means seeing if something turns out the same way many times, not just once or twice.
3. Aristotle was wrong, but people believed him. Maybe we believe some things that are wrong, too. Experimenting helps us believe what is right.
4. Modern science depends on experiments to get answers. Are there other ways to prove things right?

See how the pupil, going beyond translation, took additional meanings *to,* and derived additional meanings *from,* these passages? It seems quite clear that as one takes more and more meanings to language in print, one is able to secure more and more meanings from it.

We have talked at rather great length about reading, meaning, translation, and going beyond. Since meaning has been our central concern, we will move on to discuss more fully what we mean by meaning, and how we think it develops. Before we do this, however, we will review the major points made in our analysis of the reading process.

Summing Up

The process of reading, from the very instant one begins to learn, is essentially the process of getting meanings from language in print. Since meanings are not implicit in words, phrases, or sentences themselves, we must take meanings *to* print in order to secure meanings *from* it. This is to say that the kinds and number of meanings we get through reading depend upon the kinds and number of meanings we take to it.

As a process, reading may be thought of as involving several interrelated aspects. We may describe these as follows:

1. RECOGNIZING WORDS AND OTHER SYMBOLS. Recalling one's earlier associations between words and other symbols and the things (or people, situations, events, ideas) that they represent.

2. GETTING THE DRIFT. Developing some idea of what the material is all about, what the writer's purpose is, what he is trying to do.

3. TRANSLATING. Getting the minimal meanings, putting the substance of the materials into one's own words. Here, and in the following step, the "higher mental processes" come into play. One is thinking, reasoning, problem solving. And though one secures only the available minimal meaning, he may be said to be *reading*.

4. GOING BEYOND TRANSLATION. Calling upon acquired knowledge relevant to the material in order to secure *extended* meanings—to interpret, extrapolate, analyze, see its implications, or evaluate, or all of these. Again, one thinks, reasons, solves problems. One *reads*.

All of this, then, is the essence of our discussion. It says in detail what is contained in our definition of reading:

Reading is the process of taking meaning to, in order to secure meaning from, language in print.

If you have been *reading* what we have written so far, you should understand the central role played by meaning in reading. The meanings you take to a book and the meanings you secure from it transform squiggles on paper into history, drama, philosophy, and science, and, if you stop to think about it, this is a rather remarkable accomplishment. We need now to look more closely at the concept of meaning and how it develops, for it is far more complex than it may appear at this stage of our discussion.

Bibliography

1. Austin, Mary C., Coleman Morrison, and Associates, *The First R: The Harvard Report on Reading in Elementary Schools.* New York: The Macmillan Company, 1963.

2. Ayer, Adelaide, *Some Difficulties in Elementary School History: Contributions to Education No. 212.* New York: Teachers College Press, © 1920, Teachers College, Columbia University. Reprinted with the permission of the publisher.

3. English, Horace B., and A. C. English, *A Comprehensive Dictionary of Psychological and Psychoanalytical Terms.* London: Longmans, Green & Co. Ltd., 1958. Used by permission of David McKay Company, Inc.

4. Fraser, Dorothy M., Harry E. Hoy, and Alice Magenis, *Our World Neighbors.* New York: American Book Company, 1961.

5. Kant, Immanuel, *Fundamental Principles of the Metaphysics of Morals,* trans. Thomas K. Abbott. New York: The Liberal Arts Press, Inc., 1949. Reprinted by permission of the Liberal Arts Press Division of the Bobbs-Merrill Company, Inc.

6. Pollard, Rebecca S., *Pollard's Synthetic Method. A Complete Manual.* Chicago: Western Publishing House, 1889.

7. Progressive Education Association, Commission on Secondary School Curriculum, *Language in General Education.* New York: Appleton-Century, 1940.

8. Richards, I. A., *How to Read a Page.* New York: W. W. Norton & Company, Inc., 1942.

9. Robinson, Helen, Marion Monroe, and A. Steryl Artley, *Friends Old and New,* Curriculum Foundation Series. The New Basic Readers (2/1). Chicago: Scott, Foresman and Company, 1962. Adapted by the authors from "The Lost and Found Tree," by Ruth Lowes, in *Pictures and Stories,* November 1955. Copyright 1955 by Pierce and Washabaugh (The Methodist Publishing House).

10. Russell, David H., *Children's Thinking.* Boston: Ginn and Company, 1956.

CHAPTER III

THE DEVELOPMENT
OF MEANING

The clarity and completeness of a child's concepts are the best measure of his probable success in school learning because meaning is fundamental to such learning (7, p. 120).

You may expect us to begin our discussion of the development of meaning with a definition, but we think that to define meaning as a dictionary defines terms would do nothing but create confusion and would be essentially inappropriate. Since this whole chapter is an attempt to define meaning, we cannot do it helpfully in a few words. This is because it is the *sequence of events* in the development of meaning that determines its nature, and this sequence in every instance has its unique features, varying from person to person and from concept to concept. Any brief definition that includes all aspects of this sequence would be so general as to be useless, while to be *explicit* would be to deal with a special case only.

Meanings are not absolute. They are as varied as the people who develop them. People are unique; hence, the meanings any one person assigns to things, people, events, or ideas are unique meanings. Your meanings are like ours only to the extent that your experiences have been similar to ours.

This, then, is why we do not begin with a definition—why, instead, we will show how "communicable meanings" develop by describing the sequence of experiences that in broad outline produce meanings that tend to be similar for most people.

Before we begin, however, we need to set some limits. Clearly, we can treat the notion of meaning only fully enough to provide some major guidelines for helping children grow in reading power. There are many side roads leading off the main street of meaning—roads that you will have to explore for yourself if the development of meaning is to "come home" to you. One of the best and most interesting ways to begin is to read Stuart Chase's books, *The Power of Words* and *The Tyranny of Words* (1 and 2).

The origins of the search for meaning doubtless lie in the beginnings of time. Certainly, the very first living creatures sought meanings in their watery world, because life itself involves getting meanings from an impartial, if not actually hostile, environment. The simplest of sensate creatures must explore their surroundings for meanings so that they can secure food and avoid pain and possible extinction.

These simple explorations for meanings were (and are still) without reflection. It took man himself, and the higher forms of life, to lift the search to the level of "thought." By developing complex symbol systems—language, and especially written language—man has been able to surpass all other living creatures. Only he, through language, can derive those meanings from his relationships with nature and with other men that enable him to exercise some control over the world in which he lives.

Relating Meaning, Language, and Learning

There is an intimate relationship between language, learning, and meaning. This relationship may be expressed in the following way: Since man clearly is not born with a language, he must learn it. But he does not learn it simply to know it; he learns it in order to secure and convey meanings essential to his life as a human being. Thus we interrelate meaning, language, and learning—an interrelationship that bears strongly on the business of reading. Since meaning is at the heart of the matter, we are beginning with it and will talk about language and learning in the chapters that follow.

Our aim here, then, is threefold:

1. To observe how a child develops first-level, or direct, meanings.
2. To see how he develops higher-level, abstract meanings (both simple and complex).
3. To point out the need for exploring the nature of language and of the learning process.

As we begin our examination of meaning, we can note that growth in meaning, like human growth itself, is probably continuous. We don't really know when one phase ends and another begins. However, certain powers do appear in the child from time to time, and it is legitimate (if not unavoidable) to examine these as they appear, provided we keep in mind that human capabilities interrelate and overlap. We may add that this process of developing meanings is *cumulative*, which makes the notion of growth entirely relevant.

Development of First-Level Meanings

By watching a newborn infant search for meaning, we can not only trace its development, but we can also arrive ultimately at some notions about meaning that we think will be of real value to you in your classroom activities.

William James pointed out that the newborn perceives the world as a melange of dim sights, smells, sounds, tastes, and touches. His familiar phrase characterizes the baby's world as a "blooming, buzzing confusion." This being the case, how does the infant make any sense of existence? Indeed, why does he even try? After all, could he not just lie around waiting for care, drinking in food and sensations and doing precious little about it all?

The fact is that the baby is very much alive, and as with all living sensate creatures from the amoeba to the aardvark, something drives him to go on living as long and as fully as possible. He has all sorts of needs and drives—the various physiological and psychological forces that motivate behavior—such as the need for food, air, stimulation, security, esteem, and so forth. Of these drives and needs, the ones that eventually will interest us most are those related to intellectual activity, most easily described as *curiosities* about the world within and without.

All of these needs and drives demand that the infant act and react in order to set things straight; and, given a normal array of human capabilities, he does this remarkably well:

> He pulls away from the prick of a pin, or just thrashes about if he is very young. He clutches at objects placed in his hands, or feet. He sucks at the feel of something on his lips. He wails when hungry. Not bad for a newborn—seeking meanings already!

He is not yet concerned with remote impressions; he simply reacts to the immediate, the direct. He operates at the first level of meaning. His activities are modulated by *direct* sensations—hunger, pain, touch, sight, and the like.

> QUESTION: What idea of meaning emerges from this picture? Are these stimuli meaningful? If so, is it simply because the child perceives them? Because he reacts to them? Because he knows what causes them?

Development of Signs

As time passes, the infant begins to attend to other stimuli that do not bear directly on his bodily welfare, as do hunger and the open pin. He begins to react to his mother's song as she prepares his bottle, to the sound of his father's footsteps as he approaches the crib. At first, these were merely brute sounds or sights or touches. Now the child has begun to single them out of (discriminate among) the vast welter of impressions because, at least in part, he has noticed that *pleasant things follow:* a good meal, a soothing fondling. He has made an association so that the indirect stimuli (formerly unrelated impressions) have become signs *predicting coming events*. He reacts to these signs by behaving in certain ways, by responding in order to manage the consequences, so to speak. In anticipation, he may salivate and perhaps cry a little at the sound of his mother's song; and he will wiggle with delight at the sound of his daddy's footsteps.

In the same way, he learns to interpret countless other signs: the sight of puppy (coming, a wet kiss), the feel of his bib (coming, a good dinner), the scent of perfume (coming, Aunt Mary). But note that while he attends to many such stimuli, he continues to ignore countless others—the factory whistle, the piping of the early birds, the slap of the evening paper against the door. These stimuli are not yet associated with any consequences. Thus the child has taken the second and most significant step up the long ladder of meaning. He has developed enough associations to be able to discriminate signs.

Do you see how this second step depends on the first? Do you see how this step makes all else possible? We have described meanings arising out of direct sensations, and how, out of these experiences, certain events become signs permitting the child to anticipate these sensations. Now the child has the chance to learn to act in order to *control* these sensations. For example, feeling hunger (sensation-sign) he deliberately wails (action) for his dinner (consequence-sensation). In such ways does he build still larger units of meaning—sensations *plus* actions *plus* consequences.

In this connection, let us observe how the child establishes the meaning of, say, a ball. As a thing in the corner of his room, it has no meaning. It is simply a brute thing. But put the ball in his crib, and watch. He tastes it (ugh); he smells it (hmm); he feels it (rather soft, like my foot); and finally he throws it. In delight, he sees it bounce from the wall into his crib. Now the ball has become a sign that elicits its big, new meaning— something to throw and get back!

Again, if an infant of six months is fed milk from a red bottle and some unpleasant liquid from a blue one, he will quickly learn to turn to the red bottle when both are offered (8, pp. 87-88). Blue now means a bad consequence; red, a pleasant one.

In short the child responds to certain signs while ignoring others, and this behavior provides the key to meaning. He discriminates among a vast melange of signs largely on the basis of their consequences for him. The child (like ourselves) derives meanings from the *uses* of things, people, events, situations, ideas. The uses of things are really their consequences for him. Dewey puts the matter in this way:

> To grasp the meaning of a thing, an event, or a situation is to see it in its relations to other things; to note how it operates or functions, what consequences follow from it, what causes it, what uses it can be put to (3, p. 137).

You might test this idea on a friend. Sketch for him some weird kind of imaginary tool. Ask him to identify it. Note that whatever question he asks will produce no decisive clue until he asks how it is *used*. It will then hold meaning for him when you respond, for example, that it is a gadget for removing caps from catsup bottles. Note, also, how children define things in terms of uses: a spoon is to eat with.

In similar fashion, the meanings of war and of natural disasters, for example, depend upon the extent to which these phenomena are consequential to individuals. To some, anticipating the status of hero, war is a desirable event; to others, having loved ones in the conflict, it is a disaster. And so on through the full range of meanings that war can have.

Of course, the child's first understandings (as of ball) are limited, but in his small world most of them are quite adequate. Later, as he has more extensive experiences, he will extend and enrich these understandings through additions and subtractions, so to speak. His idea of ball will lose its specificity and grow to include the very notion of roundness, of sphericity, as in roller-bearings, balloons, gunshot, and so forth. Eventually, this concept of sphericity will provide the basis for the development of further abstract meanings in such fields as mathematics, geography, and physics, but let us keep firmly in mind that the beginnings of these abstract meanings lie in perceiving concrete uses.

Action: The Source of Meaning

Now we can make a most important point: Organisms, being alive and interacting with their environments, are actively seeking meanings. The human infant is constantly in motion when awake—clutching, crawling, testing, feeling, seeking meanings—seeking to make sense of his surroundings. Learning, and seeking meaning, are active processes native to all living things, and these very activities are at the bottom of the process of thought. If thinking is the development of meaning, and if meaning arises from discovering the uses of things, then thought must be based on action, past or present. Lewis puts it this way: "Only a creature that acts is capable of knowing; because only an active being could assign to a content of his experience any meaning . . ." (6, p. 17).

The infant, given the ball, had to act in relation to it before the ball acquired meaning. But, you might ask, can't a person simply sit and think about something—Timbuktu, for instance? To be sure. But if that person has never been to Timbuktu, and therefore has never walked, looked, or touched in that place, his thoughts about it must be based on places he *has* been—or based on pictures, which in turn are interpreted through other previous experience. And if he has never been outside his home town, his thoughts about Timbuktu will not bear much resemblance to those of people who *have* been there.

We are thus insisting that the human mind is not an organism separately endowed, existing and functioning apart from experience, apart from its environment. On the contrary, we are saying that man's mind *becomes* mind through its interaction with its surroundings, through its sense contacts with the environment.

A series of experiments by Hebb and his colleagues underscore this notion by producing substantial evidence to indicate that man must actually have external stimulation in order to maintain his cognitive processes and in order to maintain himself as an effective organism. The volunteers in these experiments were deprived to a large extent of variations in the sensations of sight, touch, and hearing. After some hours, the subjects' performances were impaired. These experiments show:

> A changing sensory environment seems essential for human beings. Without it, the brain ceases to function in an adequate way, and abnormalities of behavior develop. In fact as Christopher Burney observed in his remarkable account of his stay in solitary confinement: "Variety is not the spice of life; it is the very stuff of it" (4, p. 56).

Clearly, there is good reason to conclude that stimulation is necessary to coherent thought and perception, that is, to the process of cognition—knowing. We might venture to say that without external stimulation, meanings are distorted. But this does not suggest that meanings reside in the environment. Not at all. Meanings arise out of the actions of individuals in relation to the environment. The infant's ball took on meanings as he actively engaged with it; the narghile took on meaning as you explored its properties. In short, lacking contacts with the environment, we cannot produce a recognizable pattern of thought or plan an intelligent course of action. Therefore, what a person thinks (what meanings he secures) depends upon the nature of his contacts with the environment.

Up to this point, we have been saying that beyond the initial stage of the development of meaning—meaning that arises out of direct sensation —the child begins to develop units of meaning based on the associations that occur when he *interacts* with the environment. As we have shown, the elements of these units are the signs, his own actions, and the consequences of his actions (the resulting sensations) that are now related to each other in his mind, and the element of the units that interests and concerns us most is the *sign* component. This is true simply because our entire discussion revolves around the process of reading, which is the securing of meaning from written signs (symbols).

Time and time again, we have emphasized the notion that meaning derives from the perception of uses—the ball, the water pipe, the feeding-bottle. Unless an object (or person, event, situation, idea) is known through experience, merely associating it with a sign is never sufficient to invest it with meaning. Only when the object, or whatever, is known through experience, through interaction with the environment, can the sign associated with it take on meaning. This is such a fundamental notion that—at the risk of trying your patience—we want to restate it by way of a diagram:

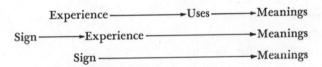

Much of the difficulty in school learning results from our neglect of the vital Experience——▶Meaning process. To be sure, this neglect is not disastrous so long as we are dealing with the kinds of objects, people, and events with which children are familiar: trees, mothers, Christmas. Moreover, if they are not familiar with such objects, people, or events, it is often relatively easy to supply the needed experiences directly. When this is not possible, substitutes such as pictures and charts can do the job at least to some degree for most children.

The signs we have described to this point are of the kind that refer only to particular objects in the child's particular environment. We need, therefore, to consider how the child moves on from the particular to the general, how he develops concepts through the process of generalizing and discriminating.

Development of Simple Concepts

Having developed certain units of meaning, the child may now apply these quite indiscriminately when he comes into contact with strange new objects and people. For instance, at first any four-legged creature is a doggy, any man a daddy, any round object a ball. Next, whether naturally or because of learning—there are still great gaps in our understanding of what happens here—the child begins to associate a sign and its meanings with objects similar to the original; he begins to generalize. But before he can be said to have attained the concept adequately, he must also be able to make the appropriate distinctions, since his generalizations may be inappropriate (albeit logical). Let's clarify this notion with an example.

After hearing his canine pal called *dog* several times, the child will ordinarily imitate the sound. Next, he will proceed to generalize, applying the label *dog* to other four-legged animals, some of which are not dogs. If his correct responses are reinforced (if he is made aware that he has used the label correctly) and if his incorrect responses are not reinforced, he will begin to perceive that there are other characteristics to be noted about four-legged creatures, some of which apply only to dogs. Finally he abstracts the notion of dog-creatures and differentiates among their relevant and irrelevant features. He will thus confidently label as *dog* any four-legged, bone-chewing, barking, tail-wagging creature. These processes, which call for both generalizing and abstracting, and for differentiating or discriminating, are the fundamental aspects of concept formation and attainment.

This uniquely human capacity for abstracting the characteristics of things is at the core of man's ability to control his environment. It enables him to make sense out of a welter of impressions, to *superimpose* form and order on a world in constant flux.

Perhaps we should note here, as a matter of interest, that abstractions do not exist in nature. They exist, as do meanings, only in our heads. Rocks, clouds, bells—all of the things of the world—have no meanings as things. It is we who give them meanings. Take, for example, the notion of roundness, an abstraction. There is really no "essence of roundness" in nature. *Round* is a label we attach to objects because they react to our manipulations in roughly the same way. If objects react differently, we may say that they are square or oblong—or shapeless! Our abstraction of the quality of roundness enables us to superimpose form on certain parts of nature, enables us to establish relationships, predict consequences, determine uses.

This is true of length, as well. There is no such thing as length in the absolute, yard-stick sense. As with roundness, length is another aspect of the behavior of things, and since we have to invent something to give form and shape to this behavior, we invent measuring devices! And as for time —would there be any time if there were no humans to measure it?

To return now to our discussion of concept development: As the infant grows, and as his world expands, he comes into contact with a variety of things that must be discriminated (differentiated) if they are to make any sense, have any meaning. This process of differentiation is vastly facilitated by his increasing power and use of language. No longer is every man a daddy, every woman a mama. These and hundreds of other labels now become true abstractions in that the child no longer applies them in a specific sense, but rather in their general or generic sense: I like *dogs;* I saw a *girl* in the store. The child can reflect about objects and events, can recall them, shift them around in his head, put them into new and different contexts and relationships, manipulate them into different situations, consider their uses.

At this point along the thinking-language continuum, two wonderful things have happened. First, the child is no longer so dependent on direct sensory experiences for meanings. Verbal signs now stand for many of them, and so they become part of his thinking process. Second, as a consequence, he can now manipulate these known symbols, relate them to other known things, sort among them, and *create new meanings.* Let us see how this might work.

Suppose the child has developed the simple concept *pencil:* "A pencil is to write with," he says. Then suppose he later develops concepts of chalk, pen, and typewriter, also as things used for writing. If he is then asked, "What can you use for writing something?" he may reply, "A pencil, a pen, chalk, or a typewriter." If he did, we could then infer that he has combined these simple concepts to make the more complex concept *writing instrument,* a new meaning.

So the child is arriving. At an incredible rate he is developing concepts —and usually the verbal signs for them—that come out of his growing ability to tell the differences among objects, people, events. This is the ability basic to the development of meaning at all levels, for just as the child determines the meaning of a writing instrument, so the learned astronomer determines the meaning of some mysterious points of light in the heavens. The child is separated from the astronomer by a quantity of experiences out of which have come the conceptions the scientist manipulates to produce meanings and new concepts, which is to say that the child's concepts are not only fewer, but are also less complex.

We insisted above on the need for direct experience if meanings are to develop, but if the child already has an appropriate set of simple concepts on which to build, substitutes for direct experience (such as pictures and charts) can often get the job done for most children. However, the matter is quite different when we get to the advanced stages involving highly abstract concepts. Here the omission of the needed experiences results in educational disaster. Observe:

Jack, how did you answer the question?

The causes of the Civil War were economic, political, and id- id- ideo-
ideo-logi-cal.

That's right, Jack. Now how many of you got this?

Of course, meaning can come later, as when we suddenly discover the
precise signification of a word or phrase we have been hearing for years,
but this hardly justifies subjecting children, through the years, to barrages
of meaningless words, words, words. Is it any wonder that some children
look upon school as something less than a citadel of learning?

Let us look, then, at the processes involved in developing complex concepts.

Development of Complex Concepts

The concepts that we have chosen to call complex are those that can
be abstracted and generalized from the simple concepts developed through
direct experience. These complex concepts stand at the center of the
educational process. A complex concept—democracy, for example—when
adequately understood, represents the interrelationships among other
concepts that may be either simple or complex. These interrelationships
may be thought of as forming a *structure* which is represented by the
symbol—usually a word—for the concept. Thus, as we move from simple
to abstract, from *tree* to *democracy*, we get involved in relationships
among concepts. We develop a hierarchy in which the abstractions are
structural, are building blocks supporting and clarifying each other. Thus
we move from the relatively simple:

tree

to the complex:

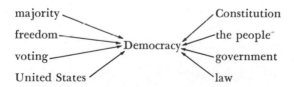

Note that although we have drawn arrows only from each supporting
concept to *democracy*, all of these concepts are nevertheless interrelated—
law and government, people and voting, freedom and Constitution. Moreover, each of the supporting concepts is in itself exceedingly complex—

freedom, for example. To draw all of the interconnections would be to transform our sketch into a veritable maze! Perhaps we should also note that for the botanist and the poet, *tree* is a complex, even ill-defined, concept!

Some of the many learning problems involved in the development of complex structures will be discussed in our chapter on learning, but before we leave the matter of complex concepts, we must point out that the child does not develop complex concepts by "synthesis" alone—by putting simpler, supporting concepts into patterns as he did to develop the concept of *writing instrument.* Just as often, he will begin with highly complex concepts that he develops as quite simple ones because he lacks the experiences that will ultimately reveal their complexity.

To illustrate this process of increasing differentiation more fully let us take the notion of *goodness,* which we as adults perceive as highly abstract and enormously complex, and which is a source of considerable philosophical controversy. What does goodness mean to a child of two? Commonly for him it is a simple concept developed out of the many times he has been told he is a "good boy," or a "bad boy." From these experiences, he has learned that when he does what mother wants, he is good; when he disobeys, he is bad. Conceptually, goodness is thus a simple notion to the child: it is doing what he is told and following the rules. It may then take years to shake such a child's conviction that obedience is the essence of goodness. In short, this concept, which for us is complex, is for the child a simple one, derived by abstracting and generalizing from a series of relatively simple direct experiences.

Gradually, however, as some of the supporting concepts—loyalty, truth, kindness, pleasure, and the like—are developed, the child will, we trust, come to see that these are all aspects of goodness. Thus eventually he will come to discriminate among these aspects, to see their relationship, not only to the concept itself, but to each other as well. Goodness for him then will no longer be a simple concept.

> NOTE: Returning to the subject of reading, you can easily perceive the significant role that reading plays in the development and attainment of concepts, both simple and complex. In societies such as ours, where so much of learning is symbolic rather than direct, reading is doubtless the major instrument by which children perceive and grow in understanding of the complexities of human existence.

The Variability of Meaning

Before concluding our discussion of the meaning of meaning, we need to mention a final, but not least, characteristic of meaning; that is, its variability. Meaning is not absolute, but is relative to (varies with) the kinds of experiences that give rise to it. Since meanings develop out of our experiences, and since our experiences differ from individual to individual, it follows that meanings also differ from individual to individual. More than this, meanings not only differ from person to person, but they vary from time to time within the same person. For example, certain words or ideas may signify particular things for a reader on one occasion and quite different things on another occasion. New experiences may produce different moods and changing expectations that often invest old concepts with new meanings.

To be sure, the degree of variability of concepts depends on the degree of complexity of the concepts involved. Simple concepts representing concrete objects—shoes and ships and sealing wax—ordinarily provide little opportunity for misinterpretation, at least visually. Unless the "interpreters" have grown up in quite different cultures, geographically, technologically, and socially, they tend to visualize such simple concepts in much the same way. Thus we visualize farm animals much as does the farmer who raises them, though we may interpret them differently. Those of us who are not farmers may see pigs as all dirt and ugly grunts, while the farmer may see them as ham, bacon, and money in the bank.

On the other hand, complex concepts—lacking as they do such concrete referents and depending for their meanings on the clarity of other concepts whose interrelationships make up their substructures—are subject to an often staggering variety of interpretations. We refer you again to our sketch of the "structure of democracy."

The results of a study involving a group of 27 students at the University of Hawaii illustrate dramatically the variability of meaning among complex as opposed to simple concepts (5). The students were presented with seven "stimulus" concepts, ranging in complexity from *color* to *cause*, and were asked to write as many terms describing each concept as they could within a stated time. Responding to *color*—a relatively simple concept—students produced a total of 186 terms, 60 of which (32 per cent) were common to three or more student lists. Responding to *cause*, however, students produced a total of 192 terms, only nine of which were common to three or more lists—5 per cent of the total.

Thus words and other symbols, ideas, people, events, concepts—*meanings*—can signify different things to different people, people who have had different experiences, who have different kinds of intellect and emotional make-up, and who cherish different expectations—all factors that go into the creation of meaning.

Summing Up

Meaning arises out of experience, which we may think of as the interaction between the organism and its environment. This is to say that meaning derives from our active engagement with things, people, events, situations, ideas. It is the interaction that reveals the uses of things, and these uses constitute meanings. Those things or people, or events, or situations that are consequential for us, that touch our lives, that affect us in some way, all have meanings for us.

As particular kinds of experiences accumulate, signs become associated with the events and with their meanings. In many, if not most cases, the sign is further associated with a word (or words), or is a word itself. The word then can elicit the meanings that prior experience has provided. Thus as language and concepts develop, it becomes possible to think, to manipulate ideas—an essential condition for reading, as we have seen.

Concepts are abstractions for which we usually have verbal signs. Concepts serve as the building blocks of thought. They develop through experience—through our interacting with our surroundings—by virtue of our capacity for abstracting the characteristics of things. Concepts may be simple, embodying common meanings derived from direct experiences with the things, people, and events that make up our daily lives and are shared by all or most members of a culture. Or concepts may be complex, high-level abstractions, referring to things, people, and events that are not "sense-able," that depend for their meanings on the clarity of supporting concepts (simple or complex) whose interrelationships make up their substructures. We think here of such concepts as truth, goodness, and democracy.

The development of verbal signs, as designations for concepts, frees the individual from dependence on direct experiences for meanings. These signs, or language-symbols, now stand for the experiences. They can be manipulated in our minds, can be related to other symbols, and can be sorted among to create new meanings. But always, to be meaningful, *concepts* (as verbal signs) *must develop out of experience*. Only when the object, or whatever, is known through experience—through interaction with the environment—can the sign associated with it take on meaning.

Because meanings arise out of experience, and because experiences differ from individual to individual, meanings differ, and the more complex the concepts, the greater the variability in meanings from person to person. This variability can lead to confusion in communication, but fortunately most people in a given community or culture have common or similar experiences, and perhaps, even more important, they have a common language whose structural characteristics limit the diversity of meanings theoretically possible, a condition that makes communication possible. Plainly, this notion is directly relevant to reading—interpreting language in print.

These and other considerations make it necessary to examine more closely the role of language in the process of securing meaning from language in print. Moreover, obtaining meaning from language in print requires a great deal of prior learning, a fact that suggests that before we can examine problems in reading instruction intelligently, we must look further into the nature of the learning process as well. Thus in the next two chapters, we will examine those aspects of language and of learning that we see as relevant to the securing of meaning. And since we are concerned with the kind of learning that is in large measure dependent on language, we turn first to a discussion of the nature of language.

Bibliography

1. Chase, Stuart, *The Power of Words*. New York: Harcourt, Brace & World, Inc., 1954.

2. ———, *The Tyranny of Words*. New York: Harcourt, Brace & World, Inc., 1938.

3. Dewey, John, *How We Think*. New York: D. C. Heath & Company, 1933.

4. Heron, Woodburn, "The Pathology of Boredom," *Scientific American*, Vol. 196, No. 1 (1957), 52-56.

5. Johnson, Ronald C., "Linguistic Structure as Related to Concept Formation and to Concept Content," *Psychological Bulletin*, Vol. 59, No. 6 (1962), 468-476.

6. Lewis, C. I., *An Analysis of Knowledge and Valuation*. La Salle, Ill.: Open Court Publishing Co., 1946.

7. Russell, David H., *Children's Thinking*. Boston: Ginn and Company, 1956.

8. Stone, L. Joseph, and Joseph Church, *Childhood and Adolescence*. New York: Random House, Inc., 1957.

CHAPTER IV

THE ROLE
OF LANGUAGE
IN READING

*A language is very like a society; we may live
long . . . in a great city before we discover
who really rules in it and on whom the behavior of which of the citizens depends (15,
p. 103).*

We have defined and illustrated reading as the process of securing and
extending meanings from language in print, and we have analyzed the
nature and development of meaning, the first of our three basic ingredients (meaning, language, and learning) that function in the reading
process. We need now to turn to the second ingredient, language, to
describe its characteristics and to show how certain of these bear on your
guidance of children's reading experiences.

We remind you here that we do not conceive of meaning, language, and
learning as functioning independently in the reading process. On the
contrary, as we have repeatedly pointed out, we find them to be intimately
related. Once again we emphasize this relationship by saying that *language*, which is *learned*, is itself a system for communicating *meanings*.
This interrelationship is explicit in almost any definition of language.
Bram, for example, defines language as ". . . a structured system of arbitrary vocal symbols by means of which members of a social group interact" (2, p. 2). To put it another way, we *learn* a system of spoken *signs* in
order to give and receive *meanings*.

Not all of the characteristics of language as language relate to the problems of reading instruction. For example, one marked characteristic is that its use is essentially automatic—one picks up a language without conscious effort. Clearly this is not true of learning to read.

Again, even the characteristic of structure, a major feature of all languages, offers little guidance. While children differ widely in their ability to manage complex relationships linguistically (to shift phrases, to subordinate ideas, to handle appositives, and the like), the vast majority come to reading instruction with a common understanding of the *basic* structure of English, the subject-verb-object arrangement of parts. Having grown up with this "kernel" arrangement, so to speak, they obey its relatively simple order automatically, and, for their purposes, quite successfully (4, p. 339).

We might point out here that investigations bearing on reading of the nature and structure of verbal learning, and especially of the psychology of language, continue to grow in number and sophistication. Thus on the one hand we have the work of linguists such as Fries (8) and LeFevre (10), suggesting how linguistics can be applied in beginning reading instruction, and on the other hand, the explorations into the nature and development of verbal behavior by such investigators as Miller and Ervin (13), Brown and Fraser (3) and Carroll (4). Recent studies of children's oral language carried out by Loban (11) and by Bereiter and Engelmann (1) suggest promising new approaches for preparing children to "decode" the printed word. We shall refer to some of these approaches later in the chapter.

With respect to the bearing of the psychology of language on reading instruction, however, the necessary comprehensive theories are lacking. As Carroll points out, "Only a new theoretical formulation can build a bridge between much of the work in psycholinguistics and problems in the practical teaching of language skills in schools" (5, p. 124).

Having noted these limitations, we will turn now to language itself to observe the full range of its characteristics. We shall present the entire range, even though, as we have indicated, not all characteristics are relevant to the business of reading. We do this to give you the full picture, so that when we turn to those characteristics that do furnish clues for reading instruction, you will have a useful vantage point. On general principle, and following our own earlier injunction, we want our discussion of the relevant characteristics to be in context!

The Nature of Language

Perhaps we can make our discussion of the nature of language clearer, or at least more dramatic, by casting it in the form of an imaginary adventure. We therefore ask you to suppose yourself to be a modern Robinson Crusoe, with only your faithful dog for companionship. Suppose further that, like Crusoe, you come one day upon another castaway who, though friendly, speaks a totally incomprehensible language. Suppose also that native pride (or prejudice) prevents either of you from undertaking to learn the language of the other. You thus settle for communicating by way of grunts, half-understood hand signals, and exaggerated facial expressions.

After several days of this kind of "pseudo-talk," pressed by circumstances, you suddenly hit upon a solution: agreement on a third language, on verbal symbols distinct from the sounds to which each of you is accustomed (we will pass over the problem of how you explained the idea!). Your companion is overjoyed at the prospect, and with enthusiasm you both set about devising your new sound system.

Day after day, you spend hours pointing to objects significant in your island environment, differentiating them with distinct sound labels. A stone becomes *glag*, water becomes *plag*, and a tree is designated by *flam*. You settle, of course, for simple sounds, easily produced by voice mechanisms "educated" quite differently.

Actions such as throwing, climbing, and washing are labeled by accompanying the action with different sounds. Thus *flim* is to climb. So far, so good: *flim flam* is "climb tree." But who is climbing, and when, and why? You find that you need additional sounds of a different order to enable you to express ideas such as cause and effect, states of being, negation, condition, and the like, as well as to make clear the traditional who, what, when, where, how, and why. Thus:

$$malgo = \text{happy}$$
$$pomalgo = \text{unhappy}$$
$$satar = \text{because}$$
$$gling = \text{if}$$
$$glant = \text{then}$$

This is an undertaking involving immense difficulties, and learning comes slowly. But come it does, and with it, better communication which in turn brings greater companionship. The refinements and elaborations of your new tongue enable you to face more effectively the physical realities of your island.

Thus you both grow in language facility and actually manage quite well. In fact, you fancy yourselves rather remarkable people to have developed so useful an instrument of communication. It is so useful, indeed, that you wonder why you revert to your original tongues whenever you try to work out plans for the future, or when you review past events. Why, you ask yourselves, with our new language, are we so dependent on our former languages in times of stress?

One day, faithful Rover comes crawling to your cave, torn and bleeding. Despite your fears, or because of them, you seize the opportunity to develop a new symbol to make clear your feelings. *"Blogir,"* you say, pointing to yourself and looking as dejected as you can. *"Blogir,"* your companion repeats, then points to himself and smiles broadly! Something obviously has gone wrong, but try as you will, you cannot invest *blogir* with the notion of sadness. We shall see why later.

For some time now you have been leaving messages for each other—little complex arrangements of sticks to indicate where, what, and how long. The day arrives, however, when the limits of expression by way of sticks are reached. Arrangements simply cannot reflect accurately enough the complexities of your activities or the necessary shades of meaning they embody. More than this, you feel the need for recapturing the events of the past, free of the distortions wrought by fading memories. So you finally come to written symbols, little dreaming that ages later, men will find on your island—perhaps in clay—a record of your existence which they will decipher for the illumination of their own.

We need not pursue what surely would be the slow evolution of your written language, involving decisions about the kind and number of "squiggles" to represent speech sounds, about what marks to use as punctuation, and the like. This much of a vignette should help us get at the nature and function of language. We have simplified a most complicated process, but essentially your island experiences with language do justice to what is known about the matter.

Now, remembering your experiences, take a moment to try to formulate some notions about the nature and function of language. It would be both fun and instructive to jot down what this vignette reveals. For example, the first point you might make is that language is man-made; you and your companion invented a language. Before reading on, try to think of some other points, and check your list with ours.

First, you and your companion did "create" a language. This suggests that there is nothing absolute about human speech. It is not a kind of sound-mirror of some over-all reality, as certain ancients believed. Rather, it is quite arbitrary and reflects, though often inaccurately, man's experiences in his particular environment. In a manner of speaking, sound symbols and their written counterparts are products of experience and can therefore mean whatever we want them to mean. All we must do to establish that *tove* signifies the pencil we write with, is to agree on it. As Bram puts it, "Symbols derive their specific function from group consensus or social convention, and have no effect whatever (outside their rather trivial physical characteristics) on any person not acquainted with such consensus or convention" (2, p. 2). So *language is a series of inventions and is thus a convention.*

Second, the fact that each of you spoke a native tongue enabled you to accomplish at once what humans before you took an unknown, but vast, number of years to accomplish—agreement on sound symbols for identifying things, events, situations. Of course you might have begun with graphic signs on bark or clay, squiggles, ideographs, or whatever, as perhaps our prehistoric ancestors did. But your prior habit of using sound symbols, plus the fact that graphic communication is impossible in the dark or from any distance, led you immediately to sound symbolism. Thus *language is primarily oral.* Written symbols seem to have followed oral expression by several hundred thousands of years (2, p. 3).

> NOTE: We do not call the cave drawings of primitive man symbols or signs, as we conceive such to be. They probably served as ornamentation rather than as representing ideas, or situations, or events.

Third, remember how you found yourselves reverting to your native tongues whenever you had to meet new situations or plan lines of attack on problems? Try as you might, you simply could not follow or elaborate a scheme successfully in "Islandese." You mixed your old and new tongues and ultimately fell back on the old to sustain thought. Why?

While there is much to be learned about the relationship between thought and language, scholars do agree that thinking is vastly facilitated by man's capacity to verbalize. At the risk of oversimplifying, we might say that since thinking is a process of manipulating symbols in order to arrive at meanings, you had trouble thinking in Islandese because you lacked the appropriate symbols to manipulate! Perhaps a little experiment will make this clear.

Suppose it occurred to you that it would be pleasant to be elected to Congress. Begin thinking about how you might accomplish this. Stop here for a moment and think about it . . .

Don't you find yourself using words such as *campaign funds, primaries, voting, party,* and the like? Perhaps you also have some purely visual images: you on the platform facing a spellbound crowd, and so on. Still, if you thought much about this at all, it is almost certain that you found words necessary to that thought.

Now imagine the problem of a person who did not have these words available. Such a person clearly could not contemplate election to Congress in any sensible way; he simply could not devise a plan that would have any reality about it.

One of the most famous students of language, Edward Sapir, tells us that ". . . thought . . . is hardly possible in any sustained sense without the symbolic organization brought by language. . . . It is best to admit that language is primarily a vocal actualization of the [human] tendency to see realities symbolically . . ." (17, p. 15).

Stuart Chase puts the matter more colorfully: "Probably everyone experiences brainstorms too fast to be verbal. In writing, I frequently have them. But before I can handle such bolts from the blue, I must verbalize them, put them into words for sober reflection, or discussion" (6, pp. vi-vii). Vygotsky sums up the matter very neatly: "Thought and language, which reflect reality in a way different from that of perception, are the key to the nature of human consciousness. Words play a central part not only in the development of thought but in the historical growth of consciousness as a whole. A word is a microscom of human consciousness" (19, p. 153). Thus *language is the chief means by which man thinks.*

Fourth, if you had analyzed the sounds uttered by your companion as he spoke your new tongue, you might have discovered that they were limited in number and that they occurred in particular combinations and sequences. For example, many of your words began with what in English we call a consonant, followed by the sound represented by the symbol *L*, such as *glag, plag, flim, flam.* On the other hand, none began with sounds represented (in English) by such symbol combinations as *ng* or *nt,* although many words ended with them: *gling* and *glant* for examples. Moreover, you might have discovered that certain sounds stood alone (*flam* = tree) while others did not (*po* = un, as in *pomalgo* = unhappy).

Thus while there is no logical relationship between sounds and the things they represent, there are identifiable relationships *within* the sound system of any language. The sounds we use in English, for example, are limited in kind and number and reveal consistencies in combination and placement that make up a phonetic system. So *language has a sound pattern.*

Incidentally, one of the major difficulties involved in learning to read English is that we utter more than forty sounds as we talk, but have only 26 symbols to represent these sounds graphically. Clearly no one-to-one sound-to-symbol relationship is possible. Thus some symbols represent more than one sound, and some symbols are combined to represent one or more different sounds. To complicate matters further, varieties of symbols are used to represent a single sound. Note, for example, the symbols used in the following words to represent the single long sound of *a:* weigh, hey, day, straight, great, bouquet.

Again, if you had analyzed your spoken tongue, you might have noted that, in addition to a phonetic system, your language revealed another interesting feature having to do with the relationship between and among sound labels. This you might have discovered in the following way. Single words often, if not commonly, sufficed for purposes of day-to-day communication. When you were hungry, for example, you could make your condition clear by saying emphatically, "Food!" But to communicate more complex matters such as, "Just as I reached the shipwreck, the storm struck," you would necessarily utter a string of words. Analyzing this series, you would have discovered that the words were not in random or chance order, "Struck the I just storm," for instance. On the contrary, they would be ordered in a particular way to make meaning clear. They would reveal a syntactic pattern, a word order. Thus *language has a structure, a grammar.*

> NOTE: In devising your new tongue, you *could* have settled on word forms which themselves contained the needed clues to relationships between and among words, as in Latin. Think of the confusion which would have resulted if your companion's native tongue had been like Latin in this respect and yours was not.

Let's return for a moment to the matter of word order. When we wish in English to express the fact that a certain Jake killed his wife, we normally say, "Jake killed his wife." We could, at the expense of style, do some rearranging and say, "His wife, Jake killed." Or we might say, "Wife? Jake killed his." These examples exhaust the possibilities if meaning is to be preserved. If, however, an ancient Roman wished to inform his listeners of Jake's crime, he could have put the words in any order he wished, even to the extent of completely reversing them: *Feminam suam interfecit Jacobus.* In fact, disregarding barbarisms and improper emphases, and using only the original four words, a Roman could have reported the foul deed in precisely 24 different ways! In Latin, as in some other tongues, meaning is established by terminal inflections, so that the *am* ending of *feminam* makes Jake's wife the undisputed victim no matter where she stands in the sentence.

Modern students of English, unlike their predecessors to whom grammar was sacred and immutable, agree that language cannot be considered a "set of fixed rules and principles, a logical structure of rules . . . which govern speech and writing" (14, p. 274). Unfortunately, most earlier investigators undertook to regularize English by basing their grammars on the Latin system. That is, they attempted to describe our language in terms of the structure of Latin, a language with which they were familiar and which they held in veneration as a model for all language. This approach not only provided a very bad picture of English but, what is worse, resulted in the notion that there are absolute and logical "rights and wrongs" of expression that have to be observed if one is to be proper and understood.

For example, classical grammarians, noting that Latin has six tenses, insisted that English have six. The fact is that English has but two—a past and a present. Moreover, because Latin is full of case distinctions, they saddled us with such notions as nominative, genitive, and accusative cases. Yet English, except for the possessive, has no case distinctions what-soever. As for propriety, if there is nothing absolute about language, who is to say what is really right and wrong in expression? Correctness is sim-ply a matter of accuracy in meaning, and of sociology—of agreement upon usage.

Fifth, remember the incident of wounded Rover and your vain effort to invest *blogir* with the notion of sorrow? Disconcerting as was your companion's continued smiling, his response was quite in keeping with his upbringing. He could not associate *blogir* with sadness simply because his culture had taught him to look at the death of loved ones quite dif-ferently. Death was not to be feared or wept over; rather, it was to be accepted and even welcomed as the release from the cares of life and the beginning of eternal bliss.

Sapir and Whorf, among others, tell us that language develops in and through and out of a culture, that it does not reflect some universality of human thought and feelings and logic. It reflects instead all of the con-ceptions and misconceptions about man and nature that result from man's relationships with nature and with other men. In short, language develops out of the way men perceive the world and relate to it; the way men perceive the world and relate to it is reflected inexorably in the lan-guages they use. It seems that before man can rearrange his way of per-ceiving the world and its events, he has to rearrange his symbol system, his language (16, Ch. 10; 20, p. 252).

Whorf devoted years to the development of Sapir's thesis that thinking is conditioned by the language one speaks (20, pp. 207-219). The Greeks, after Aristotle, on the other hand, assumed a great, universal framework or umbrella of logic that language reflects or expresses. So they thought that different languages were simply different ways of expressing this universal logic.

Linguists and anthropologists have discovered fascinating examples of how environment, hence language, conditions man's ways of thinking about his world. The Hopi Indians have no designation for time as a single concept; no word for time exists in Hopi. The conditions of Hopi life have not made our concept of time necessary. For this reason, as Whorf points out, the Hopi think always about events in terms of space-time, and can therefore visualize the notion of relativity more easily than can we language-bound speakers of English (20, pp. 57-58, 216-217).

Again, as Dorothy Lee discovered, the Trobriand Islanders use no adjectives (2, p. 15). When the quality of an object changes, they simply give it a new name, which appears to be a marvelous way of avoiding the fallacy that is sometimes inherent in the notion of identity, a notion that our intransitive verb *to be* builds into our language: A *is* A. In reality, nothing in the world is the same as it was a split second ago (people, especially!). But we habitually talk and act as though it (and people) were. This is a dynamic and rapidly changing world; it is not the dependable world of the ancients. And the Trobrianders appear to have recognized this, while we have not. At least, their language permits action more in harmony with immediate reality than ours does!

These examples should help us realize that there are really no "primitive" languages in existence. The tongue spoken by even the most "backward" people is highly complex, capable of carrying incredibly fine nuances of meaning. Sapir points out that "The lowliest South African bushman speaks in the forms of a rich symbolic system that is in essence perfectly comparable to the speech of the cultivated Frenchman" (16, p. 22). Understanding such languages requires years of on-the-scene study by expert linguists.

In this connection, the American linguist Whorf points out the hold that patterns of language (ways of "chopping it up") have upon our very thinking:

> . . . the forms of a person's thoughts are controlled by inexorable laws of pattern of which he is unconscious. . . . And every language is a vast pattern-system, different from others, in which are culturally ordained the forms and categories by which the personality not only communicates but also analyzes nature . . . channels his reasoning, and builds the house of his consciousness (20, p. 252).

Thus a sentence such as "I see the sky," Whorf points out, makes one think of an infinity of cosmic gas in the same way one thinks of a relatively isolated body such as a rock or a planet. Does one really *see* the sky? Does one *get* an idea as he *gets* a blow on the head?

Notice further that mathematicians, to escape the strait jacket of language, use a relatively new language, the calculus, that enables them to get away from our three-dimensional world into space-time. Much as we like to think that we are masters of our mother tongue, we are in many ways still its slave. There is

> . . . a kind of relativity that is generally hidden from us by our naive acceptance of fixed habits of speech as guides to an objective understanding of the nature of experience. This is the relativity of concepts, or as it might be called, the relativity of the form of thought. . . . It is the appreciation of the relativity of the form of thought which results from linguistic study that is perhaps the most liberalizing thing about it. What fetters the mind and numbs the spirit is ever the dogged acceptance of absolutes (17, p. 159).

There are other interesting aspects. How many of us really sense the failure of our language to describe the events of nature as modern physicists, say, understand them? Nature is continuous, in truth. Events flow without break into other events. There is no true beginning point, no identifiable ending point. But our language (which must *describe* nature) is not continuous at all. It requires that someone, or something, *do* something. In this respect, Whorf calls our language *bi-polar*.

For example, we say "It is raining." But in nature, *it* doesn't rain. The phenomenon of precipitation occurs, as pure action, but our language won't permit us to describe pure action (natural phenomena) as such. We have to tack on a noun or pronoun to make the action work! Accordingly during a storm we may say, "It is lightning," while the Hopi say far more accurately, "Rehpi"—flash! (20, p. 243).

The fact is that we can't define an event from nature; we have to do it by getting back to our grammatical categories. We are blinded to the realities of nature by the bi-polarity of our language.

Clearly, in many ways, we are the prisoners of our illogical tongue. "The great disease of knowledge," says Ivor Richards, "is that in which, starting from words, we end up with them" (15, p. 162). And we can only conclude, in the absence of conflicting evidence, that "The fact of the matter is that the 'real world' is to a large extent unconsciously built up on the language habits of the group. . . . We see and hear and otherwise experience very largely as we do because the language habits of our community predispose certain choices of interpretation" (17, p. 162). Thus *language shapes our thinking*.

Now let us turn to a consideration of several additional characteristics that are essentially extensions of the five we have just described. For the sake of clarity, we are grouping these extensions under two headings: those that are *social* in nature, and those that are *psychological* in nature.

Language and Society

The fact that language was invented by man makes clear the idea that *language is a cultural phenomenon*. Alone on your island, you had no practical reason for speech. Rover was most uncommunicative—verbally! But the appearance of the castaway made communication significant and necessary for the purpose of efficient conjoint enterprises. Although the precise origins of speech are still matters of conjecture, its social function is clearly established. Dewey, for example, puts the notion thus: "The primary motive for language is to influence (through the expression of desire, emotion, and thought) the activity of others" (7, p. 239).

Now since language is a cultural institution, it changes with the passage of time in the same way other cultural institutions change. That is, *it is subject to change as people, things, and situations change*. Thus *palgo* (shipwreck) might gradually drop from your speech simply because this ancient tragedy grew less important, even in memory. Verbs would become more precise, and some words would take on totally different meanings. Your *blogir,* for example, might lose its sense of sorrow and come to signify joy, as your companion originally interpreted it.

Historical changes in word meaning can be a fascinating study. See, for instance, what happened to the Middle English *seli* (blessed). By the end of the fourteenth century it meant *simple;* and today it is the word *silly.* From the sublime to the ridiculous in 700 years!

People occupying different sections of the same country usually speak in a dialect because of geographic isolation, environmental differences, and what is known as "linguistic drift." These lead to differences in ways of life, and these in turn lead to language variations. Thus *language is culturally localized.*

Moreover, since most "civilized" societies come to some divisions of labor in order to "produce more and better," these divisions produce class distinctions—workers on the one hand and managers on the other. And class distinctions lead to language differences. Those engaged in certain occupations develop new symbols that enable them to work together more efficiently, to reflect their particular ways of life. Thus *language is marked by social layers, by stratifications.*

These social layers differ mostly in terms of vocabulary, and there are lesser differences with regard to sound and structure. Your messenger boy, for example, would certainly understand *flim* and would pronounce and use it as you did. But *grensado* (double-entry ledger) would probably never occur to him, much less pass his lips!

Finally, with the passage of time and with the increasing complexity of your society, the need for more efficient ways of thinking and behaving would probably bring social institutions into being. A system of education would evolve; religion would become formalized and would be practiced in houses of worship; a governmental structure would form; fraternal orders would emerge; the military would come into existence; and professional and labor groups would develop.

Each of these elements, both accidentally and by design, would develop a particular "lingo" that people would adopt and repeat until finally the symbols would all but lose meanings. Yet the patterns of speech would develop, and people would wear them more like skin than like clothes. To get along in a group would require that one use the words and phrases common to that group. Thus *language becomes standardized.*

Language probably resists change more fiercely than custom itself. Have you ever become uneasy at the persistent repetition of verbal ritual, say, on the Fourth of July or even in church? Many have, but it is probable that the same people would feel a good deal more uneasy *without* some sort of ritual!

A second major aspect of language as a social institution has to do with the relationship between its spoken and written forms. You recall that your written language developed some months or years after your spoken language. In the meantime, you and your people had begun to distort and even eliminate many of the older words. You no longer said *blo-gir* and *gren-sa-do,* but more casually, *blugger* and *grensdo.* Yet these changes did not appear in your books or dictionaries. Moreover, many words in your written language, no longer heard in common speech, still appeared in written form. Again, you and your companions began to use "modern" words and expressions which your lexicographers did not think common enough to include in their compendiums. Hence, normally, *changes in written language follow changes in speech.*

> NOTE: It is true that, as changes occur, the conventions of written language need not exactly or even closely parallel the conventions of speech. Either or both can change independently. For example, we point out the differences between vulgar and classical Latin which, by the sixth and seventh centuries, had become so marked that lexically and structurally, spoken and written Latin were hardly the same tongue (9, p. 4).

Perhaps this sort of thing wouldn't happen in a society in which everyone was literate and did a lot of reading!

The Psychology of Language

In this section, we leave those characteristics of language that derive from its social nature and turn to those that relate to its psychological nature—the manner in which language is used by the individual. In a way of speaking, we turn from describing its use by *men* to describing its use by *man.*

We have already agreed on two principal characteristics that are psychological in nature: not only is language the vehicle of thought, but it also conditions thinking. In short, we have said that there is an intimate relationship between language and thought, a relationship that manifests itself in the two ways discussed below.

Language, in the final analysis, accompanies every human action. It is the reflection of an individual's total personality—thoughts, actions, attitudes, feelings. Going about your daily affairs on the island, for example, you were aware at times that language, spoken or unspoken, flowed constantly. You were without it only when you slept—and perhaps not even then! Perhaps it is not too much to say that language is part of all behavior. Thus *language is all-pervasive; it reflects one's whole personality.*

Again, on the many occasions when you reverted to your native tongue to think out projected actions, you did so quite unconsciously. Your habit of thinking in your native language came to consciousness only when you found yourself mixing languages, which required conscious probings of memory. You used your original language, however, without thinking about it as such. Thus *our use of language is usually without conscious effort.* We do grope for words on occasion, and we often deliberately try out ways of phrasing things, but our use of language is largely automatic.

These, then, are the several characteristics of language as language. We are now ready to identify and discuss in some detail the two of these that bear on the process of reading and provide us with useful clues to more efficient reading instruction. These characteristics are those that relate (1) to language as an invention, hence as a convention; and (2) to language as primarily an oral phenomenon. It may well be that some of the other characteristics bear on the process of reading, but if this is so, the relationship has not been identified.

Language as a Convention

As we pointed out earlier, sounds and written symbols were invented by man in order that he could communicate. Thus words are simply signs (symbols) *representing* things, people, ideas, events. They are intermediary, standing between us and the things they represent. John Wilson expresses this notion well when he writes:

> . . . although we do not perceive 'things' and then invent one label for each 'thing,' we do perceive similarities in our experience. . . . If the same experience occurs often enough to make it worth our while, we invent a word or sign to use on any occasion when we wish to communicate the experience. We see that pillar-boxes, poppies, and stop-lights are similar in one respect: and so we use the word 'red' to express this similarity. We perceive that certain things are all small, circular, and hard; and we invent a noun for the occasions when we wish to speak of any of these things, the noun 'penny' (21, pp. 20-21).

In short, words are not independent entities having existences of their own, a fact that we made clear in our discussion of meaning. Words are verbal labels man has "made up" so that, as Wilson points out, he can talk about things, can communicate thoughts, desires, feelings.

Now of course this is all well and good—verbal symbols enable us to work and play together effectively and fully (usually!), hence to function adequately together. But our habit of affixing verbal labels, our practice of "naming" things, commonly leads us into a linguistic trap, a trap that children must be helped to avoid if they are to become the kind of readers we want them to become. This trap takes the form of a subtly and gradually developing belief in the "omnipotence of words," a belief that some maintain arises during the early stages of children's language learning, when they realize that they can manipulate the behavior of adults through the use of words (2, p. 20). Bram describes the dangers of this linguistic trap:

> This infantile belief [in the omnipotence of words] persists through the person's whole life, and, combined with other factors, accounts at least partially for several important behavioral phenomena. The latter include, for example, the widespread use of language in magic (in the form of spells, incantations, ritual formulae, and so on); the well-known human inclination to substitute words for action; the tendency to ascribe "thingness" to purely mental constructs and abstractions such as *culture, conscience,* and *love* (known as reification); and the exceedingly common irrational belief whereby things and their names are related to each other in a natural, necessary, and inseparable manner (2, p. 20).

In the context of the classroom, then, we commonly find children visualizing words as things, as some kind of tangible entities rather than as representatives of highly complex concepts that need to be thought about (if not experienced) *as such,* to be understood.

> This is *justice* . . .
> Here we have *government* at work . . .
> See how *love* wins the day . . .

Here the written words, like spoken ones, often get in the way of meanings. Because we have labels for concepts, they tend to be visualized as tangible, unchanging entities, and we don't bother to examine them.

The habit of confusing symbol with thing leads children (and "unreconstructed" adults) to accept as quite logical such statements as "The Divine is rightly called," and "Pigs are properly named because they are so dirty."

Another danger, perhaps even more serious, generated by this belief in the power of words is that of mistaking words for action, of thinking that they can substitute for deeds. Unless we are conscious of this danger and take pains to sensitize children to it, our pupils soon learn to rest satisfied with mere talk, especially in the seductive (if not soporific) forms of rituals and ceremonial codes and "I promise's." And we do not exclude from this category the youth organization pledges, patriotic oaths, and religious petitions whose purposes are precisely to stimulate socially desirable behaviors.

A final, and most serious, danger inherent in our belief in the omnipotence of words is our susceptibility to verbal persuasion, our unconscious responsiveness to, or rejection of, symbols that experience has rendered either near and dear or frightening. We are all familiar with this phenomenon in connection with what students of propaganda call "emotionally freighted" words and phrases such as *mother, country,* and *patriotic duty* on the positive side, and *atheist, Big Government,* and *totalitarianism* on the negative. Terms such as these, spoken and written to enlist support for, or opposition to, all manner of causes, commonly substitute for rational arguments and appeals.

As we describe this problem in connection with the conventionality of language, you may be thinking of it in connection with speech rather than with language in print. If so, you are wondering about its relevance to the reading process. Our view of the matter is that while belief in the magic of words doubtless arises in the context of oral language, it begins to transfer to written language from the moment the child learns his first printed words. Confusing spoken words with things, he goes on to confuse written words with things; beguiled (or deluded) by oratory, he tends to be equally beguiled by written persuasion; satisfied by repeating slogans and rituals, he becomes satisfied by reading them.

To help children escape the danger of confusing word with thing, we suggest "dis-associative" activities designed to make clear their independence. These would include helping children to invent new labels for old things, to make up and communicate in a "new" language, to note that seeing or hearing symbols (*tree, cat*) is not the same as having the referent bodily at hand, and so on. Basic to the effectiveness of all such activities is the notion that we must constantly hammer home—the notion that "This is *not* a pennant . . . or pencil . . . or chair," but, "It *is* a piece of red cloth we *call* a pennant . . . something to write with *called* a pencil . . . something to sit on *called* a chair . . ." and so on.

To help children avoid mistaking words for action, the danger inherent in verbal rituals, slogans, and ceremonial codes, we suggest leading them to "spell out" the kinds of behavior implied by such utterances. For example, at the simplest level, "What might we *really do* if we wanted to be 'good citizens' in our room, and why?" (Here we would take care that the spelling-out is realistic in terms of what physically energetic children can and cannot be expected to do during a long school day. We do not look kindly on the traditional "Good Citizen" chart which suggests that the good citizen is one who never whispers or leaves his seat without permission.)

At a more sophisticated level, "What might we *really do* if we wanted to be loyal to our family . . . our friends . . . our school . . . our city . . . ?" Again, children must be helped to analyze all kinds of writings—speeches, debates, advertisements—to see how language is used to persuade, entice, and delude for both useful and harmful purposes.

Finally, we mention two other practices that are observable in one form or another in most written language and that are also conventions: (1) the arrangement of graphic symbols (in English, left-to-right and top-to-bottom) and (2) the use of nonverbal symbols—punctuation marks and certain mechanical devices—as substitutes for gestures and for vocal cues to meaning. Many children need considerable practice to establish the habit of left-right eye movement across lines of print, and all will require instruction in learning to interpret punctuation marks and other devices as clues to meanings in print. In the following section we will further discuss these nonverbal clues to meaning.

Language as an Oral Phenomenon

When we stop to analyze oral expression in general, and children's speech in particular, we discover that it reveals two marked characteristics, neither of which is a feature of written language. First, it is accompanied by a variety of nonverbal cues that make meanings clear, and second, it is the primary expression of thought; written language is secondary, once removed.

The existence of these differences between speech and writing means that unless we transcribe exactly the words of a speaker, language in print is really not "speech wrote down," as the boy in the fable put it. Although we are not as badly off as the sixth century Romans mentioned earlier, we do not have a one-to-one correspondence between oral and written language, especially in the language of children's literature (texts and trade books). Hence children who are learning to read are encountering what is—to the extent of these differences—a new language. For this reason, we need to describe these differences more fully.

As for our first characteristic, when we speak of nonverbal cues to meaning, we refer to gestures, to facial expressions, to body posture, and particularly to three major vocal cues: stress or emphasis, pitch, and pause. While these cues are not ordinarily thought of as part of language itself, they are such inseparable and universal concomitants of speech that we may consider them to be so.

Without these nonverbal aids to meaning, much of our speech would be ambiguous, if not unintelligible. For instance, to appreciate the function of stress as a determinant of meaning, say aloud, "They are cooking apples." Stress *cooking* for one meaning; stress *apples* for another. To note the importance of pitch and pause, say, "Woman without her man is a savage." Drop your voice and pause after *man* for one meaning; do the same after *woman* and *her* for quite a different meaning.

Our second characteristic, the fact that our speech directly reflects our thought processes, accounts for three marked features of oral expression. *First,* rather than being compact and orderly, it is loosely organized, unsystematic, and often even chaotic. Thus, like thought itself, speech is marked by repetitions and rephrasings, by fresh starts, by omissions of words and phrases, by superfluous expressions, and often by meaningless wanderings and language fragments. This is illustrated by the following descriptions, by two boys, of incidents occurring on their favorite TV programs:

> Superman, I seen him last night . . . Clark Kent in Superman, do you know? An he, an he puts an aspirin, you know, a bad man puts the aspirin in this little . . . in here, an, an he said, and this guy, well he told him . . . (11, p. 58).
>
> I saw a hunter program last Sunday an he, an snow time he had to have a lot uh, wah-h when he, uh, not too many dogs, he . . . and that's all I think of that picture (11, p. 9).

Nor is such disorganization to be heard only in the speech of children and youth. Here is an "educated" adult as we transcribed him:

> Sure, I . . . well . . . he wouldn't make any . . . I could see he had no intention . . . um . . . of coughing . . . you know, paying me back.

Second, the speech of all but the most verbally gifted individuals is characterized by a high degree of simplicity. This is to say that essential meanings are commonly expressed in basic or "kernel" form, uncomplicated by such grammatical and rhetorical strategies as we find in the language of books: prepositional phrases, infinitives, appositions, verbals, figures of speech, and especially subordinate constructions, the vehicles for conveying delicate nuances of meaning (11, p. 85).

Now when we characterize oral speech as simple, we are not contradicting what we said earlier about the disorganization of most oral expression. Speech can be, and commonly is, at once loose in form and simple in pattern. As "wandering" as is the boy's description of the Superman program, it is expressed in a basically uncomplicated subject-verb-object pattern. Omit the irrelevancies, and we have:

> . . . I seen him . . . he puts an aspirin . . . a bad man puts the aspirin . . . he said . . . he told him . . .

Third, all spoken language reveals cultural and class influences. How people express themselves depends on where they live and how they live, on what social class they fit into. Grammar, pronunciation, vocabulary, phraseology, and style differ more or less widely from area to area and from class to class. Few are those who speak in "standard" English, which is itself a class dialect. Observe some common variations from standard speech:

REGION	MODES OF EXPRESSION	
Standard English	small portion	cow
Cumberlands	smidgen	cow-beast
Smokies	canch	cow-brute
Blue Ridge	tiddy-bit	she-cow

(12, p. 361)

And "listen" to a native of the Ozark region:

> Lee Yancey allus was a right work-brickel feller, clever and biddable as all git-out, but he ain't got nary smidgen o' mother wit, an' he ain't nothin' on'y a tie-whackin' sheer-crapper noways (12, p. 359).

Thus man and child speak not only as they think—in fits and starts— but also as their culture and class speak.

As man struggled through the centuries toward some way of representing speech graphically and devised symbols to stand for sounds, these two characteristics must have given him pause. As for the first, if nonverbal cues are essential for communicating meanings in spoken language, they—or something like them—are essential to written language. Since written symbols can neither gesture nor speak for themselves, the answer had to lie in the notion of "something like them." Thus were invented punctuation marks and certain mechanical devices (such as the underline, the upper- and lower-case letters, and the like).

> NOTE: These substitutes are unnnecessary in languages that utilize written signs to depict ideas rather than words. For example, Chinese writing is ideographic; its written form has no connection whatsoever with speech sounds, hence requires little punctuation.

Returning to our earlier examples, we may stress by underlining either *cooking* or *apples,* depending on the meaning we wish to convey. As for the pauses which give different meanings to our pronouncement about woman and her man, we can represent these graphically in several ways:

Woman? \
Woman: \
Woman— } without her, man is a savage. \
Woman!

Or of course we can favor the man and write:

> Woman without her man, is a savage.
> Woman—without her man—is a savage.
> Woman (without her man) is a savage.

As for our second characteristic—that having to do with the "looseness" and relative simplicity of speech—there is no logical reason why we should not transcribe speech verbatim, provided of course that it is intelligible. Let us return to our young admirer of Superman and add two words to his utterance, but preserve his structure:

> Superman, I seen him last night . . . Clark Kent in Superman, do you know? An he, an he puts an aspirin, you know, a bad man puts the aspirin in this little (bottle) . . . in here, an, an he said, an this guy, well he told (Superman) . . .

Despite its informality, the statement is now quite clear: I saw Clark Kent in Superman last night, and a bad man put an aspirin in a bottle and said to Superman . . .

But as our observant ancestors discovered, writing something exactly as it is spoken usually makes for very tiresome reading. Wordiness, repetitions, fresh starts, irrelevancies, and even wanderings, soon discourage all but the hardiest of readers. Moreover, stark simplicity of expression, though often refreshing from the pens of experts, commonly cannot transmit the nuances of meaning that are inherent in human relationships, in ideas, and in situations and events. Finally, our system of language taboos decrees that whatever is written for children (at least) be free of all profanities and most vulgarities.

As we write, therefore, we recast our thoughts, we rearrange sequences and polish up our grammar, we search for more appropriate words and phrases, we subordinate to impart more complex meanings, and, for the sake of clarity and propriety, we eliminate localisms, profanities, and vulgarisms—except those relatively innocuous expressions needed for color. In short, we write in "standard" English—formal, compact, logical, and socially acceptable:

> I saw Clark Kent as Superman last night. Well, in order to get Superman in his power, a certain bad man put an aspirin in a bottle, then said to Superman . . .

So each of these differences between speech and writing sets a special task which children must somehow manage in order to deal effectively with language in print. All must learn to interpret punctuation and mechanical clues to meaning; all must adjust to a more precise and compact mode of communication; many, if not most, must come to terms with standard English, a language different grammatically, lexically, and stylistically from their own speech; and all but those with superior language power must learn to make sense of a subtler, more complex way of expressing meanings.

As we pointed out at the beginning of this chapter, there is considerable evidence that the greater children's skill in oral expression, the more successful they will be as readers. After a study of the speech of 338 children as they progressed from kindergarten through grade six, Loban concluded that "Competence in the spoken language appears to be a necessary base for competence in writing and reading." And he adds, "It would be difficult not to conclude that instruction can yet do more than it has *with oral language*" (11, p. 88).

The findings of investigators working with the so-called culturally deprived child strongly support Loban's conclusions about the child's need for adequate oral-language skills before he comes to language in print.

Silverman, reporting the consensus of participants in a recent conference on the education of the culturally deprived, writes:

> Adequate auditory and visual discrimination are necessary for successful speech development and for learning to read. Children from lower-class homes have been found to be weak in auditory discrimination and visual discrimination at the beginning of school. The range of oral vocabulary possessed by lower- and middle-class pupils has also been found to differ. In particular, lower-class children lack abstract language—words for categories, class names, and non-concrete ideas . . .
>
> To learn words, children must try them out in new situations and receive correction and extension of their vocabulary and ideas (18, p. 70).

Similarly, the research of Bereiter and Engelmann demonstrates the usefulness of extensive practice in oral expression in helping deprived children compensate for their language deficit so that they can work at their school learning tasks more effectively (1).

In the light of all this, then, we propose that the instructional program include a wide range of learning experiences designed to bring children's speech into closer correspondence with language as it is conventionally written. The more children can be helped to think and speak like, or at least to anticipate the unique features of, language in print, the better prepared they will be for the new modes of expression it embodies, the better prepared they will be for managing the tasks we have outlined. In essence this means that we need to help children get and give meaning via "pure language," reducing reliance on nonverbal cues (pointing, facial expressions, emphases, and the like). What we are after is strengthened ability to use and understand language alone.

We do not suggest that current school programs in the language arts lack scope and depth. Indeed, such programs involve a vast array of "tried and true" techniques designed not only to improve children's skills in speech and writing, but also to sharpen their ability to listen more effectively. What we *are* saying is that there should be special attention given to the problems arising out of the *differences between speech and writing*, to the end that children may come to reading more easily and naturally. To do this calls for an addition to the traditional instruction in the arts of verbal expression in general and the skill of reading in particular.

This addition involves dealing with children's oral expressions and helping them to think about and analyze their own speech, with a view to saying what they want to say more effectively—more compactly, more systematically, more meaningfully. We find Loban's conclusions apt:

> Since formal instruction in grammar—whether linguistic or traditional—seems to be an ineffective method of improving expression at this level of development, one can conclude that elementary pupils need many opportunities to grapple with their own thought in situations where they

have someone to whom they wish to communicate successfully. Instruction can best aid the pupils' expression when individuals or small groups with similar problems are helped to see how *their own* expression can be improved. This instruction would take the form of identifying elements which strengthen or weaken communication, increase or lower precision of thought, clarify or blur meanings. For the pupils, the approach would usually be through models, meaning, and reasoning rather than through the application of rules (11, p. 88).

Thus, for example, middle- and upper-grade pupils might take turns describing to their classmates how something "works"—a doorbell, flashlight, or even a narghile! Their explanations could then be discussed ("critiqued") by other pupils. If tape recorders are available, explanations could be transcribed for study and editing by the children involved or by a committee, perhaps for inclusion in a class "How It Works" book.

Younger pupils, as individuals or in groups small enough to ensure that each child is actively responding, may be helped through word games to develop a number of language skills and understandings. For instance, to bring informal oral expression "into line with" formal written expression, teachers may have pupils reply in complete sentences to questions such as "What is Jane doing? What is Jack wearing? What is her (pointing) name?" and the like. Pupils would then be helped to respond "Jane is sitting down. Jack is wearing glasses (or a red sweater). Her name is Alice."

To help develop children's perceptions of spatial relationships, the "Where is it?" game may be arranged. Here, a child stands before his small group and holds or places a book (or other object) in various positions with respect to his body. Classmates respond in chorus (and in "complete sentences"), "The book is on his head . . . under his arm . . . under his feet. The book is in front of Jack."

A wide range of such language-development activities are described by Bereiter and Engelmann (1). Although they have been prepared for preschoolers, many may be adapted for use by older children.

Summing Up

We began our discussion of the role of language in reading by emphasizing again the intimate relationship among the three basic ingredients of the reading process: meaning, language, and learning. Then, in order to provide a complete context, to paint the full picture of language, we described a number of characteristics of language, even though only two bear directly on learning to read:

Language is man's invention, hence is a *convention*.
Language is primarily an oral phenomenon.

With respect to the first, to say that language is a convention is to say that verbal symbols have no independent existence, no meaning *per se*. They are simply the signs for things, people, ideas, relationships, events, stiuations, and the like.

While such signs are necessary—we need them to communicate effectively—they very often get us into unexpected and unrealized difficulties. These difficulties stem from our tendency to conceive of words as things, to confuse labels with the things they represent, so that they get in the way of our seeing and dealing with the realities of our environment. We are thus seduced by the magic of words so that we permit them to take the place of action. Hence a major goal of reading instruction is to help children avoid this linguistic trap, to help them put symbols in their places, so to speak, and to help them *get* meaning, not lose it.

With respect to the second characteristic, because language is primarily a spoken phenomenon, there are features in its spoken representation not observable in its written form. Hence children coming to reading need to be prepared to manage the features of written language that differ and contrast with spoken language:

1. The compactness and precision of form.
2. The greater complexity of expression.
3. The greater propriety of substance and style.
4. The grammar of standard English.
5. The punctuation clues to meaning.

There are steps that can be taken to prepare children to manage the problems posed by these two characteristics of language. One procedure would be to use exercises directly designed to dissipate the power that words have over us. For the other characteristic there should be exercises utilizing children's own expressions as the bases on which to build a closer correspondence between speech and language in print.

We turn now to learning, the last of the three basic ingredients of the reading process.

Bibliography

1. Bereiter, Carl, and Siegfried Engelmann, *Teaching Disadvantaged Children in the Preschool.* Englewood Cliffs, N.J.: Prentice-Hall, Inc., 1966.
2. Bram, Joseph, *Language and Society.* New York: Random House, Inc., 1955.
3. Brown, Roger, and Colin Fraser, "The Acquisition of Syntax," and "Explorations in Grammar Evaluation," *The Acquisition of Language,* Monograph, the Society for Research in Child Development, Vol. 29, No. 1, 1964.
4. Carroll, John B., "Analysis of Reading Instruction," *Theories of Learning and Instruction,* Yearbook 1963, Part I, National Society for the Study of Education. Chicago: University of Chicago Press, 1964.

5. ———, "Language Arts and Fine Arts," *Review of Educational Research,* Vol. XXXIV, No. 2, April, 1964.

6. Chase, Stuart, "Foreword," reprinted from *Language, Thought, and Reality: Selected Writings of Benjamin Lee Whorf* edited by John B. Carroll by permission of The M.I.T. Press, Cambridge, Massachusetts. Copyright 1956 by the Massachusetts Institute of Technology.

7. Dewey, John, *How We Think.* Boston: D. C. Heath & Company, 1933.

8. Fries, Charles, *Linguistics and Reading.* New York: Holt, Rinehart & Winston, Inc., 1962.

9. Grandgent, C. H., *Vulgar Latin.* Boston: D. C. Heath & Company, 1908.

10. LeFevre, Carl A., *Linguistics and the Teaching of Reading.* New York: McGraw-Hill Book Company, 1964.

11. Loban, Walter D., *The Language of Elementary School Children,* National Council of Teachers of English, Research Report No. 1. Champaign, Illinois: The Council, 1963.

12. Mencken, H. L., *The American Language.* New York: Alfred A. Knopf, Inc., 1937.

13. Miller, Wick, and Susan Ervin, "The Development of Grammar in Child Language," in *The Acquisition of Language,* Monograph, the Society for Research in Child Development, Vol. 29, No. 1, 1964.

14. National Council of Teachers of English, the Commission on the English Curriculum, *The English Language Arts.* New York: Appleton-Century-Crofts, 1952.

15. Richards, I. A., *How to Read a Page.* New York: W. W. Norton & Company, Inc., 1942.

16. Sapir, Edward, *Language: An Introduction to the Study of Speech.* New York: Harcourt, Brace & World, Inc., 1921.

17. ———, *Selected Writings in Language, Culture, and Personality,* ed. David Mandelbaum. Berkeley, Calif.: The University of California Press, 1949.

18. Silverman, Susan B., "An Annotated Bibliography on Education and Cultural Deprivation," in *Compensatory Education for Cultural Deprivation,* ed. by Benjamin S. Bloom, Allison Davis, and Robert Hess. New York: Holt, Rinehart & Winston, Inc., 1965.

19. Vygotsky, L. S., *Thought and Language,* ed. and trans. Eugenia Hanfmann and Gertrude Vakar. New York: The M.I.T. Press of the Massachusetts Institute of Technology, and John Wiley & Sons, Inc., 1962.

20. Whorf, Benjamin Lee, *Language, Thought, and Reality,* ed. John B. Carroll. New York: The Technology Press of the Massachusetts Institute of Technology, and John Wiley & Sons, Inc., 1956.

21. Wilson, John, *Language and the Pursuit of Truth.* Cambridge, England: Cambridge University Press, 1956.

CHAPTER V

A LOOK
AT LEARNING
AND INSTRUCTION

Learning to read is not learning to know something; it is learning to do *something (5, p. 186).*

We shall begin our discussion of the role of learning in reading by stating the obvious: one must learn to read, and the mature ability to read is the product of long sequences of learning. A great many specific things must be learned and these must be combined into general patterns that are related to the language, the knowledge, and the thinking of the reader.

We have talked at great length in preceding chapters about what a child is learning when he learns to read. We now offer a brief set of assertions about learning and instruction—the *how* rather than the *what* of learning to read—that we hope are extensive and relevant enough to contribute substantially to your understanding of the problems of teaching reading.

Most discussions of teaching—and the teaching of reading is no exception—bear only a vague relationship to present knowledge about learning. Certainly the most hotly argued matters about methods or approaches to teaching reading do not involve arguments about the learning process as such. Rather, they are arguments about what should be taught (whole words, letters, syllables) and when, about what materials to present to the student and how they should be arranged.

Most of the psychological propositions that have been used in these arguments turn out to be two-edged swords, because the issues do not

ly involve specific instances of individual behavior. And individual behaviors—actions with specific antecedents and consequences—are what psychologists study. Hence extrapolations to assertions that leave specific behaviors ambiguous are not likely to be very clear or very helpful.

The point of all this is that what we have to say about teaching is meant to be limited to specific student behaviors and those specific teacher behaviors that may elicit this student action. To avoid confusion with the "methods" argument, we will call the latter teaching *techniques*.

We will divide our discussion of learning and instruction into two major parts. In the first, we will present a series of propositions about learning and instruction. In the second, we will reconsider the meaning of these propositions in light of the fact that these are abstractions and we are dealing with human beings.

Learning and Instruction

Below we offer seven propositions about learning and instruction. For the sake of clarity, we present them in one-two-three order.

1. *Teachers cannot learn for their pupils; it is the actions of pupils that determine what pupils learn.* Note that by actions we mean not only talking, walking, and other physical movements, but also feeling, thinking, and reading.

To say that the actions of pupils determine what they learn is to say substantially what Dewey said decades ago, that pupils learn what *they do*. What *you* do or say may be termed "teaching," but it is only what the pupil does or thinks or feels that is "learning." Of course it is true that any activity on your part may result in some kind of pupil activity (whether overt or covert, good or bad). But the trick is for you as a teacher to act so that what you do produces the pupil activity you want to see—which may then produce the kind of learning you are hoping for.

Having been a student for many years, you undoubtedly remember long stretches of school time during which your teacher's activities apparently affected you not at all ("What did the teacher do? Gosh, I don't remember!"), also some that affected you positively ("I never knew poetry could be exciting till I heard him read yesterday."), or adversely ("Why doesn't she quit talking about that boring stuff?"). But even in the case of the poetry student, if that is the end of the matter, the teacher failed. However, if the student then reads some poetry on his own, or tries for the first time to discover the meaning of a poem, or starts to write poetry, *then* the teacher's action of reading aloud accomplished something because the student took action—he did something relevant.

In any case, this first proposition suggests that if you want the appropriate learning to occur, you need to get the pupils involved with whatever is to be learned. You will recall we emphasized this notion when we talked in Chapter Three about experience (doing and being done to) as the source of meaning. So if, for example, you want the young reader really to understand spatial relationships in print, you do not stop with telling him that "Under the house is the basement" and "Over the house is the roof." You have *him* put an eraser in the "basement" of the model house as he says "Under the house." And you have *him* hold the cotton bird above the model as he says, "Over the house." And thus also with *beside* the house, *front* of the house, *back, near, outside, inside, next to, away from, around* the house! The young reader is doing—and learning. And "next to the house" in print will take on real meaning.

Remember that your *intent* that he learn means nothing; it is what *you get him to do* that counts. And if he does not do what you want him to, you cannot let it pass. Your task is to get him to do it. Only *after* the student has done the thing you wanted is it reasonable to expect that he has learned something of what you set out to teach him.

2. *What a student does depends on his set.*

We think the concept of set is an important and potentially most useful one for a teacher in planning and devising techniques.

> The external elements in the learning situation combine with the needs, abilities, and prior learning of the student to create an internal state we will call a *set*. Set determines what cues the student perceives as relevant and determines his strategies or ways of going about the task as he sees it (6, p. 60).

Set, then, is a kind of predisposition to see, hear, or otherwise perceive things and people and ideas in one way rather than in another. It is to get from situations certain meanings that we are "predisposed" to get, and to ignore or overlook other meanings. For a simple illustration: The trained observer finds the abstract painting an interesting and exciting composition; the untrained observer is repelled by what to him is a lack of form and order. These two people really see two different things because of differences in their set, created here by prior learning.

Teachers deliberately manipulate pupil set in order to influence learning. But they also influence pupil set unwittingly all the time, and these unwitting influences, interacting as they do strongly with the personality of the pupil, often create undesirable sets which get in the way of learning. We think that this point is so important that we will devote the last half of this chapter to helping you be more "witting"! For now, we wish to limit our discussion to the largely intellectual (cognitive) as opposed to the emotional (affective) factors in learning.

With respect to intellect, set is largely a function of:

> a. The external cues present: the learning materials, the teacher's instruction, and the other pupils present.

b. The pupil's previous learning: his general habits of proceeding, his skills, and his knowledge, insofar as he perceives them to be relevant.

And since meaning is a function of set, "reading readiness," for example, may be thought of as the degree to which the parts of the learning task are meaningful to pupils. The parts here depend on how the teacher decides to proceed, thus controlling readiness. For example, if the teacher decides to begin reading instruction by having children learn the names of the letters, obviously those children who know that there are such things as letters are "readier" than those who don't. Again, because some children seem to have an ear for sound, they are "readier" for a phonic (or synthetic) approach than are the children not so endowed, who may be "ready" for a whole-word (or analytic) approach.

Readiness was once viewed as a natural unfolding of capacities and thus was treated as an element of set beyond the teacher's influence but about which he was supposed to have been informed so as to act at the proper time. More recently readiness has come to be viewed as largely learned, and "readiness activities" are now usually part and parcel of the learning activities which are meant to create the appropriate set for the next task.

In short, we believe you will find the notion of set a useful one because it points to all the elements in a situation you need to consider as a teacher and, as you might have guessed, it makes meaning one of the central elements.

3. *What a pupil sees as relevant depends on the meanings he brings to and derives from the learning materials.*

In this sense, reading itself is like learning. You will recall (how can you forget?) that we defined reading as taking meaning *to,* in order to get meaning *from,* language in print. Learning, also, is the process of taking meaning to a situation in order to derive meaning from it. Reading is thus a special case of learning—it is learning in a very particular kind of situation. In short, learning to read is a special case of learning to learn!

Also the aspect of learning we are discussing is the heart of the classic psychological problem of education: the transfer of training, of which learning to learn (or the formation of learning sets) is the aspect of most concern to teachers. As a teacher, you are (or will be) most concerned with helping pupils develop effective ways of learning. That is, you want children, when faced with a learning task, to proceed in effective ways to accomplish the task. And since reading is one major part of many of these ways of learning, it should be very useful to talk about the business of *learning to learn.* In specific instances we will call this the formation of a learning set, since the psychological condition to which we refer predisposes a person to learn a certain specific kind of thing quite rapidly.

The formation of a learning set involves long sequences of learning, and we must consider some additional propositions about learning and teaching before we can pursue the matter.

4. *Teaching techniques consist of telling, showing, and reinforcing.*

We would remind you again that we do not intend to pursue the various arguments about methods. Nevertheless, some discussion of technique, as defined on page 58, is certainly in order.

If you listed all the possible direct teacher behaviors meant to produce children's learning activities, you would find that you could put each of them under one of the following:

a. Telling pupils what to do (providing a verbal model):
   "First, look at the first letter. Now look at the last . . ."

b. Showing pupils what to do (providing a physical model that pupils can imitate):
   "Watch how I fold the paper." (folds long way)
   "Now like this." (folds again)
   "Now once more." (third fold)
   "What do you have?"

c. Letting pupils devise their own models, and then providing reinforcement for correct responses:
   "Here is a list of words. Tell me what you notice about them. That's right, they're all nouns . . ."

This is the sum of the business of techniques, though it is hardly all there is to teaching! These basic techniques can, of course, be augmented by the use of various devices such as films, computers, books, and tapes. Moreover, the teacher can arrange for others to perform any or all portions of his task for him. For example, he can have other pupils perform them or other teachers (via televised instruction perhaps). Of course, the learning activities of the pupils can be varied endlessly.

NOTE: A technique, unlike a general approach or method, is not something to be followed over a long period of time. The purpose of a technique is to get the pupil to *do* something, and effective teachers are constantly shifting techniques—often by the minute. It is common for them to be using more than one technique simultaneously, as with two or more children or groups of children.

But bearing in mind that teachers cannot learn *for* students and can only try to influence their learning activities, the three categories presented above are exhaustive.

With respect to the first category (*telling* children), teachers, for the most part, cannot usefully tell children how to read. During some early phases of learning to read, it may be useful to say to the child, "Look first at this letter, then this letter." But usually this procedure is of limited value. Hence the first technique plays a small part in reading instruction. One does not give first graders lectures on how to read and probably should not do so very often with high school students either.

In the second category (*showing* children, providing models) we have a highly useful procedure for the teacher who is centrally concerned with *meaning*. Over and over again, opportunities arise to provide children with models of how to read, not only how to read aloud, but also how to follow plot, interpret character, draw inferences and conclusions, and so on. Thus you may "talk through" the material as you read aloud, pointing out various aspects of the material that need emphasis or clarification. By describing aloud the sequence of thoughts aroused by stories or articles, you can help pupils realize that these thoughts are part of reading. Pupils can thus see what sorts of connections, inferences, and extrapolations are possible and appropriate during the reading process.

To use this technique successfully requires great skill and substantial knowledge and understanding of pupils. That is, one must take account of both the degree of intellectual development and the experiences children bring to the classroom. One aspect of children's intellectual development to take into account is the degree to which a child can work with relationships among abstract ideas. For example, given several apparently unrelated facts, can he develop a reasonable generalization—can he "put two and two together," so to speak? Again, can he extend a concept such as "fair play" in games to the more general and elaborate idea of "liberty and justice for all"? One way to mitigate the problem is to see that insofar as possible verbal symbols develop out of (are tied to) real things, and that interrelationships among symbols are explored. You may recall our discussion of this in Chapter Three.

As for children's experiences, the skillful teacher knows that there are differences between the meanings brought to school by the suburban middle-class child and by the inner-city slum child. For instance, we are reminded of the response given by an eight-year-old inner-city child to the question, "How do our senators and representatives get their jobs?" The child, recalling his father's job-seeking activities, replied, "They go down to the employment office and fill out a paper." Thus when he wants to supply models (show how) that have appropriate meaning, the teacher needs to avoid depending on meanings unavailable to the child.

As for the third category (letting children devise their own models and reinforcing correct responses), if pupils are active and doing any of the appropriate things, all that is needed is reinforcement of those elements of the pupils' activities that the teacher hopes to perpetuate. This technique is probably the one most used in teaching reading, because, as we have pointed out, there are many elements of the reading process that we do not really understand. Hence we can neither *tell* pupils what to do, nor provide models of how to do it. Instead, we encourage them to try, and we reinforce those trials appearing to go in the right direction: "Good, Jack. You got the word," or "That's right—you stopped when you came to the period!" So we reinforce correct responses by praising, rewarding, providing feedback, providing knowledge of results, or however one chooses to describe the process of reinforcement.

5. *Reinforcement is a central part of the learning process.*

The basic idea here is that when something like a reward follows a response, that response is strengthened or reinforced; that is, it is more likely to reappear (it is being learned). If it is not reinforced, it becomes less likely to reappear (it is being extinguished). Research on the concept of reinforcement has established that to be effective it must be prompt, if not immediate. Moreover, it must appear frequently, although not invariably.

You can readily see that a teacher who undertakes the task of ensuring prompt reinforcement of most of pupils' responses has a very difficult task even with very few children. And when you consider that reading is a long sequence of responses occurring in rapid order, the task becomes seemingly impossible. It was with this in mind that teaching machines and programmed instruction were developed.

Finally, many of the controversies about reading revolve around differing conceptions of just what constitutes a response in reading, that is, about what the unit of learning is—the letter, the grapheme, the word or phrase or sentence. Thus there are believers in the "phonic" approach, the linguistic approach, the whole-word approach, and so on. In any case, reinforcement of correct responses requires knowledge on the part of the teacher of whether the response is in fact correct. In even a brief time, the task of analysis can get very complex. Hence the teacher must have a very clear notion of just what the pupil should be doing and what role any given response, however defined, plays in pupil learning. In sum, the teacher has the task of supplying reinforcement within a second or two to a rapid sequence of responses that he can't always identify for each of thirty children simultaneously. What a pickle! We shall call this the teacher's dilemma.

But in order not to leave you with this dilemma, we suggest a threefold solution. First, you must take care to deal with each pupil individually as often as possible, regardless of how you group them. It is true that most teachers view individualizing instruction as important, for they complain a great deal about being unable to spend time with individuals. Perhaps our present form of school organization—predominantly the self-contained classroom—does make individualized teaching appear difficult, but we are inclined to think that, for one reason or another, many teachers are not really very eager to devote any considerable time to individual children. If they took seriously the fact that learners are always individuals, and not groups, they would begin:

    a. Setting up private sessions while others pursue assignments.
    b. Utilizing self-help devices and self-directed exercises.
    c. Using the technology available, such as programmed materials, individual film projectors, and so on.
    d. Scheduling small-group remedial periods.
    e. Using pupils in "each one help one" activities.
    f. Arranging with colleagues for team teaching which can free one or more teachers for individualized or small-group instruction.

Those teachers who have instituted a program of individualized reading will perforce be doing many of these things. For descriptions of this approach see Veatch (14), Lazar (8), or Darrow and Howes (3). We do hope you take seriously the importance of working with individuals. If you do not, you will probably not profit much from the material that follows.

Second, you must try to get pupils to provide their own reinforcement by ensuring that they bring sufficient relevant meanings to language in print to derive meanings from it. For, so far as we know, understanding anything has a rewarding effect on all humans. Here again, we are suggesting that to deal effectively with the complexities of reinforcement, you must focus persistently on getting the pupil to understand, must do everything in your power to help the pupil comprehend; as long as your pupil is deriving the appropriate meanings from his reading, reinforcement is taking care of itself and *you* can concentrate on ensuring that the other conditions of practice are met.

This does not mean that you should (even if you could) ignore the component skills of reading. It simply means that you must make securing the meaning of the material your primary and basic aim. Please bear this in mind as we turn to the third solution which does concern the component skills of reading and which will eventually get us back to the formation of learning sets. So far we have talked primarily about learning something once, but this third part of the solution to the teacher's dilemma is based on two further points about learning which concern learning to do something *well* (point six) and *learning to learn* (point seven).

    6. *Repetition or practice is at the heart of learning any complicated material or skill that consists of many parts.*

You undoubtedly have heard warnings against mere "rote practice." These warnings are appropriate unless the practice meets certain conditions, two of which are important.

The first one, feedback, we have already discussed. The child needs to know whether he is doing the right thing; he needs to be able to assess his progress; and, when he comes to language in print, he needs to *secure meanings from his efforts*. Although we have now said this often enough to convince you that we consider it important, stating the idea and using it in practice are two different things. We are not claiming that this condition is always an easy one to meet.

The second condition is easier to meet. Each practice trial should differ from the others in its nonessential elements. This is the difference between rote practice and practice that helps one discriminate between the relevant and irrelevant features of a situation. For example, the child is likely to develop erroneous and limited idea of cats if they are always associated with people, houses, and wicker baskets. The essential aspects of cats as a class of animals tend to be confounded with irrelevancies, so that, unless they are connected with humans or human artifacts, tigers, lions, leopards, and bobcats may not be viewed as cats at all. Again, as we suggested in Chapter Three, any four-legged creature is *doggy* to the toddler until, by viewing a variety of four-legged animals, he is led to see that there are other characteristics to be noted about four-legged creatures, some of which apply only to dogs. So he abstracts the notion of dog-creatures and differentiates among their relevant and irrelevant features.

In fact, one of the principal activities you will be engaged in as you try to help children develop meaning is to point out to them the existence of and differences among the various relevant components of the learning materials. Note that this is the technique of telling and is obviously helpful in dealing with the *content* of reading.

What does practice accomplish? First, as learning proceeds, you will notice less variability in the child's approach to his materials. This means, for example, that during the initial stages of learning to read, the child will stop holding his book upside down and will look from left to right along lines of print instead of wandering all over it with his eyes. Most teachers fail to notice such reductions of variability as a result of practice simply because they think only in terms of *right* and *wrong* responses. Hence when, as often happens, the child is learning the wrong thing, the teacher fails to recognize this as learning and concludes that the child is failing to learn. Not at all!

While learning the wrong thing is certainly not what we want, it is *learning* just the same and is a far cry from failing to learn. The typical reason for learning the wrong response is just that the nonessential elements have not been sufficiently varied. Thus the child who has learned to deal with capital letters only as they "begin sentences" and who does not have a set to first *seek meanings*, is likely to pause in his oral reading when he meets a proper name, thinking he has completed a thought. Of course the solution is to call the child's attention to the meaning suggested by the materials. You could *tell* the child not to pause until he spots the "period–capital letter" combination, and he might learn this. But this approach is in the long run less effective than focusing the child's attention on meaning, so that the period–capital letter combination is seen only as a device, as a secondary cue to meaning.

Reduced variability in the response patterns elicited by a situation is the hallmark of learning, just as variability in behavior in new situations is the hallmark of an intelligent approach to learning. In short, performance improves with practice. We probably did not even need to say this, but it may help to emphasize the second outcome which is less self-evident.

The second outcome of practice can be seen only if the practice is continued well beyond the point where one can claim the material is learned. If, for example, practice ceased after a child had first learned to "sound out" a particular word, you would never see the change that occurs as the child encounters that word a number of times in reading. Think of the difference between the painful and odd-sounding way a child sounds out a word the first time and the way you pronounce it: "E–man–sip–pay–shun" (same emphasis on each syllable) says the moderately skillful child seeing the word for the first time. The chances are that if you run into the word *muliebrous* for the first time, you will do better, but not as well as you do with emancipation!

All of this adds up to the blending together of parts learned separately into larger and more functional wholes. When something is practiced frequently enough, the parts begin to lose their distinctiveness. They then no longer are seen as units and do not elicit separate responses. The sequence of behaviors which are the separate parts of a complex performance such as reading become more or less automatic and rate the label *skill*. You can see that as skills develop, the number and variety of responses of a pupil which need to be reinforced become sharply reduced.

This, then, is another way of reducing the difficulties we have labeled the teacher's dilemma. But we must expand this idea of repeated practice if we want to show how the dilemma is more than mildly mitigated.

We shall do this as our next point. But we will suggest here that as this practice-after-learning proceeds (you may have recognized the description of "overlearning") and formerly discernible parts lose their identity, some potentially serious pitfalls can be created. If the child now encounters learning situations that demand new arrangements (and meanings) for these "lost" parts, he may have great difficulty. Thus if inappropriate learnings are practiced to this point, it may be almost impossible or at least extremely difficult to change. For example, you may have encountered the difficulty of getting someone to alter some improper use of language to which he is accustomed. The problem is not one of *intent*, but simply of the whole response (improper use) being run off before he is aware that the error is included in his expression. It can be a real big, or rather a really big problem!

We may now turn to our final point in this section.

7. *After long practice skills tend to become organized into stable patterns or abilities.*

This idea takes us back to our third point, sets and the development of learning sets. Not only can repeated efforts lead to the development of specific skills, but eventually, as a number of related skills are developed, we may begin to talk about learning sets and abilities. Many, if not most, of the learning sets relevant to reading are language habits and styles of thinking. An adequate list of these habits is not available since, as we pointed out in Chapter Two, a satisfactory description of the reading process in more than general terms is not yet available. Still, we may guess at a few and suggest that some of them may be:

a. The eye movements appropriate for reading.
b. The visual discriminations involved in identification of words (not their meanings) and sentences and other written language patterns.
c. The phonic translations (sounding-out) that identify some new words.
d. The many different language skills involved in getting meaning from a sequence of words once identified.
e. The many different sets of knowledge and ways of thinking brought to the particular material being read.

The development of these abilities (learning sets) is usually slow, but once learned, they are rarely if ever forgotten. Have you ever met anyone who has forgotten how to read? However, you doubtless have encountered, or surely will encounter, people who have not developed all the needed skills and habits.

These habits take a long time to develop and require many attempts. Hence you must take every opportunity to get pupils to practice the specific single habits, and this often requires that you give explicit step-by-step directions. If inefficient or faulty habits develop too far, they are very hard to change because they have become automatic (again, the child who paused in his oral reading every time he spotted a capital letter). You cannot afford to let pupils deficient in reading proceed without direct help, unless the *meanings* the pupils are deriving from their efforts clearly provide them with this guidance.

We should caution you, however, that whenever you do something for a pupil when that pupil is capable of working it out for himself (when he can judge the appropriateness of his own activity), then you are robbing the pupil of an opportunity to practice just those habits that are the most useful. To avoid this consequence is difficult, but clearly the way to minimize it is constantly to draw the pupil's attention to the *meaning* of the learning material. By so doing, you reduce the amount of direction you need to provide and increase the amount of pupil practice of the basic skills.

The pupil who obeys the "capital letter" signal probably has not clearly gotten the idea that reading is *first* a matter of getting meaning and, after that, the pause, the stress, and the pitch can come naturally. Rules of punctuation, then, can be viewed for what they are—not rules to be obeyed apart from meaning, but simply conventional adjuncts *to* meaning.

Remember that it is not what you do but what the pupil does that counts. It follows that the more time the student practices reading rather than listening to you, the more rapidly he will improve. Because to some degree most pupils have incompletely developed habits and/or less than maximally useful habits, it is usually possible to help pupils develop better habits if you provide practice:

    a. Under conditions that enable pupils to understand and *accept* the purpose of the activity so that it will be meaningful—relevant to some goal.

    b. In circumstances where you (or better, the pupil) can ensure that the conditions of practice that we have mentioned are operating.

    c. In adequate amounts; that is, for a long enough period of time, frequently for several months.

This discussion of practice and the development of learning sets is meant to help you see once again that meaning is not only the goal of reading, but also that it must be a part of the learning process, even at points where other aspects of the task, such as practice, are the center of attention. Although frequent practice sessions over long periods of time are important if fluency is to develop, attention to meaning is vital every minute of the time. Otherwise that time is misspent, and the learning (of course there will be *some*) will not be what you are looking for. Instead, pupils too often will come to dislike reading and to believe it is a waste of time or, what is worse, that they cannot succeed at the task.

Since these feelings and attitudes are widespread in our schools, we will turn next to the emotional (affective) side of learning. First, however, let us sum up what we have said.

Pupils learn, teachers don't (they really do, but you know what we mean). Therefore what pupils do does matter, and what you do is important only insofar as it produces pupil activity. What pupils do is a function of their set, and the teacher is only one element—often a small one at that—in determining pupil set. The teacher is not the center of the stage in learning, especially in the case of reading.

Teachers can tell pupils what to do or can show them how to do it, but much of the time their role should be one of encouraging and supporting those responses of the children judged appropriate. The last of these is probably the most important role for teachers to play in many kinds of learning, but especially in reading. Yet this is not a simple role, because the rapidity and obscurity of the responses to be reinforced makes it difficult with even one pupil, much less with a roomful.

The solution to this difficulty involves, first, the individualization of instruction; second, constant attention to meaning at all levels and at all stages of learning to maximize self-reinforcement for each pupil; and third, a great deal of practice which, if properly designed, will eventually produce an approach or set that enables the pupil to proceed without further help.

The Freedom to Learn

The ability to read is made up of many specific skills and sets organized in patterns that eventually become related to each other. One of the organizing elements in the ability to read is an aspect of set we haven't yet discussed, because up to now we have dealt with the intellectual and symbolic factors involved in learning to read. We have talked very little about the teacher-child relationship and about how and why we must take the child himself into consideration as we guide his growth in reading.

Now this "intellectual approach" would be quite proper if learning were wholly, or even largely, a matter of intellect, if the human organism had only intellectual needs, and if the mind operated independently of emotions. Indeed, if children could put aside all distracting or negative feelings and simply "learn to read," the problems of instruction would be almost negligible. Imagine thirty children in a classroom doing absolutely nothing except "pure learning" for six hours—no bodies, no feelings, just solid cerebration!

But all this runs counter to the facts and is obviously fantasy. Thoughts are never just "pure thoughts," untainted by feelings, developed out of some cold, self-winding intellect. On the contrary, the act of getting at meanings is brought about by feelings and, in turn, produces feelings. The very way we perceive a thing is a function of the way we *feel* about it:

> One should not confine the concept of meaning to ideational responses. Having the different words "thinking," "feeling," and "doing," leads us to talk about behavior as if it were sometimes one and sometimes the other of these three. It is more likely that at practically all times our behavior has all these aspects (13, pp. 75-76).

So the mind is all of a piece, and feelings are not just intruders to be cast out. They arise out of experience and actually determine meanings; they *are* meanings. Feelings, experiences, meanings go hand in hand. As we discussed meaning in an earlier chapter, we saw that:

> The meaning of a thing or situation to a person is in his attitude toward the thing or situation. The meaning is the way he feels about it, or how he reacts to its presence. Meaning, in short, is his personal response. A person's response is his experience with a thing or situation (15, p. 200).

Thus if a child has had bad experiences in the reading circle, then the circle *means* to feel unhappy, among other things. In this sense if he has been embarrassed by his teacher in the presence of others, then teacher *means* someone to dislike or fear. If he has been successful in his early manipulation of numbers, then arithmetic *means* enjoyment. He feels bad or he feels good about things and situations; these feelings are part and parcel of the meanings they hold for him.

> NOTE: During our discussion we will not talk explicitly about values, with which the school is properly concerned. The notion of value is implicit in the attitudes of children toward whatever they do. If they feel good about a thing, they tend to value it. We want reading to *mean* satisfied curiosities and the pleasure of discovery, so that children will value it.

Now perhaps you will think we are going too far the other way. Perhaps you are conceiving the notion that children are nothing but bundles of feelings—no intellects at all. Let us hasten to remind you that all living organisms try to know and to understand their environments. In an earlier chapter we talked about this "reaching out" that the infant engages in, in order to comprehend and manage his small world. So we are saying here that these efforts to understand lead to experiences that result in feelings. These feelings are built into the meanings of things and, in turn, shape the nature of subsequent experiences.

Among these feelings is an omnipresent meaning—a child's feelings toward his world (the meanings it holds for him) which are a function of his *feelings about himself* (what he means to himself). Feelings about self constitute an element in learning. Perhaps we can rephrase the matter in this way: children get meanings out of situations in terms of how they feel about those situations, and how they feel about situations is colored strongly by how they feel about themselves.

Maslow, among others, suggests that while all children have needs to know, unless they perceive themselves as worthwhile and adequate, unless they esteem themselves, they are simply not genuinely free to know and to understand, to see things as they are, undistorted by fears, anxieties, and tensions (10, pp. 90-91). Combs says:

> We are even discovering that a child's success in school depends in very

large measure upon the kind of self-concepts he has. . . . More often than not, when a child is unable to read, the difficulty seems to lie in the fact that he has developed *an idea about himself* as a person who cannot read (2, pp. 22-23).

Of course it may well be that in many instances the reading difficulties develop first and, when solved, then become a force toward a more adequate self-concept. However, this does not alter the fact that negative expectations about one's self can become self-fulfilling prophecies.

By acting upon things and people and in turn being acted upon, the infant learns to differentiate himself from his world as an independent something that can make things happen. He comes to know, to develop a mind, to be conscious of "self." He develops a *me*. As we said earlier, making appropriate discriminations is the first and central step in developing meaning. The discrimination between *me* and "out there" is one of the first ideas that humans develop.

Awareness of self inevitably involves feelings and attitudes about self, and the nature of these feelings and attitudes is essentially determined by the kinds of experiences the child has. Moreover, it is especially determined by the way *others* respond to his behavior, to the way he looks, and to what he says and does. To stretch a figure, the child's picture of himself is a picture taken with someone else's camera. The child experiences himself, as Stone and Church put it, "indirectly, in the way the environment echoes his behavior back to him; he learns to see himself through the world's eyes" (12, p. 115).

Now what is important in all this is that the child who does not esteem himself, in a sense sees through a glass, darkly:

He often cannot be objective about situations seeing them as others see them, because he is preoccupied with isolating and eliminating what he perceives to be threats and dangers.
Or when he does anything right, he often does it for the wrong reason: "I'll show him up . . . I'll prove I'm right . . . I'll get back at them . . . I'll prove I'm just as smart . . . I'll do it and then he won't hate me."
Or he refuses to try anything because he sees himself as a chronic failure.

McCandless points out: ". . . poor self-concepts, implying as they so often do a lack of confidence in facing and mastering the environment, will accompany deficiency in one of the most vital of the child's areas of accomplishment—his performance in school" (9, p. 270).

This is our real concern as teachers. Often such a child is simply not free to attend to the full range of meanings inherent in the reading experiences we plan for him. He is not emotionally free to learn. Too many of us still cling to the ancient notion that if the child wants to learn, he will learn. If he doesn't learn, it must be his fault or stupidity, and we can fairly turn our attention to those who do want to learn, to those already successful. Of course, many children do learn without any attention to these matters on the part of their teachers. These fortunate ones have found the world a warm and friendly place and have learned to like themselves and others. Perhaps because some children are free to learn, we are fooled into thinking that all children are. This is the dream, not the reality. Clearly, we need to take into account the way children feel about themselves and the world as we guide them in their search for meaning through reading.

Unaware of the central role of feelings and attitudes in learning, the school of yesteryear held education to be largely a matter of mental training by way of "mastery" of the subject matter of instruction. It had little concern that the studies be useful to or valued by children, or that the subjects be selected and taught with a view to the needs and feelings of children. Nor was the school concerned with children's motives or values. Indeed, it was held that values could not really be taught; they were simply "acquired." Thus it did not worry about how children felt about school, about the courses of study, and, least of all, about themselves. In fact, the more distasteful the subject to be studied, the more educative, because it demanded greater effort of will which strengthened that faculty, promoted habits of self-reliance, and increased the power of concentration. "It makes no difference what you teach a boy," Mark Twain said acidly a century ago, "so long as he doesn't like it."

Most schools of yesteryear were formal and academic, and the teachers as teachers (as earlier portrayers of the school scene have made clear) were unconcerned with children's schoolroom feelings, needs, attitudes, and values. Teachers enlisted attention by threat and promises of punishment, and if neither worked, they solved the problem simply by eliminating the offenders. At their worst, they were drillmasters, the Gradgrinds and M'Choakumchilds of the Dickens novels. Now, although schoolmen no longer subscribe to this theory of mind training, many teachers still work with children in ways that suggest the theory has not been altogether discarded.

How often do we find novices, as well as experienced teachers, struggling day after day with some "slow" children to get them through their drills—to learn sight words, or to master initial consonant sounds, or to recognize root words. "If they would only pay attention!" these teachers say plaintively, if not bitterly. What a waste of time, and really, what a waste of human resources! Many of these are not "slow" children; these are troubled children, bored, or afraid, or tense, or anxious, or uncertain of themselves. How *can* they pay attention? Such children need less pushing and pulling, more affection, more understanding, time to grow less uncertain, less tense, less anxious, and above all, they need activities that have meaning to them so they can understand, and so they can see progress toward goals they accept. But what do they too often get if drill fails? More drill or more punishment, open or disguised.

Attention to children's feelings does not necessitate our becoming amateur psychiatrists, social workers, and agents of legal action. We have neither the time nor the skills to help every child adequately solve his out-of-school problems. We cannot improve unhappy home conditions, put love in the family circle, reduce destructive parental pressures, or reorganize a child's whole way of looking at himself and the world. These are conditions commonly far beyond our powers to change.

On the other hand, most teachers are in a position to set the emotional tone in their classrooms. This tone must be one in which children are emotionally free to learn. Most teachers accept this idea. Why, then, do we find classrooms like those we have just described? There are two common reasons why we—teachers—often fail to let children be free. The first is our habitual use of threat with its concomitant punishment. Its use is often habitual because it seems to work immediately and is therefore reinforced frequently. The second is our usually unwitting attempts to perpetuate dependence on our authority (often by threat!) because of the satisfaction this "control" gives us. Let us consider threat first, then its concomitant punishment, and finally the problem of dependence on authority.

THREAT

Nothing is potentially more disastrous, educationally speaking, than threat used to ensure obedience and attention. It can be a disaster for the teacher if it fails and a disaster for the child if it succeeds. Let us dispose of the first of these briefly.

If you threaten a child or a group of children without the will or the way to follow through, sooner or later (usually immediately) the emptiness of the threat will be realized, and in most instances you will lose control of your pupils. In fact, your threats may well become a signal for disorder or lack of attention or whatever, simply because pupils will realize that you are expecting such, and people tend to act as "important others" expect them to act. Clearly, then, if you must threaten, you must make the threat realistic and you must follow through most of the time. This is often even worse for the pupils, since, sad to say, many teachers seem to have no lack of imagination in presenting convincing threats to pupils.

Before discussing the consequences of threat to pupils, we believe that it is necessary to describe carefully what we consider threat, because it can be a tricky business open to substantial confusion and misunderstanding. By threat we do not mean that which follows a child's perception of the natural consequences of an action over which he has control. There is no threat involved when a child, for example, learns that he cannot ordinarily break the laws of nature and escape pain. He is not threatened by a hot stove after a hand-burning experience because he knows he can control the situation. He is afraid of burning his hand again but not of the stove. Nor is it threatening to point out to children, or otherwise lead them to see, the possible consequences of actions whose courses they are unable to see for themselves.

Moreover, it is not threat to let a child see the relationship between his progress and his efforts. Note that we said the relationship between his *efforts* and his *progress;* that is, let him make his own judgment of his achievement. Again, there is no threat in holding children to realistic classroom regulations which they can see are clearly needed to ensure good working conditions.

But threat *is* involved when teachers manufacture unpleasant consequences (punishments) in order to secure effort, if not interest. Unfortunately, so much of what children are asked to learn in school is so little related to their daily living and so lacking in imaginative appeal, hence so meaningless, that teachers, despite the best of intentions, resort to all manner of threats: loss of privileges, detentions, nonpromotion, test failure, rejection by friends and parents, and so on. For example:

> What in the world is your Daddy going to think of your reading when he comes to Back-to-School Night? I'm sure he will wonder what on earth we have been doing for a month. Now let's . . . Of course you needn't worry about these weekly tests. Of course you can fail them. Just remember, though, that report cards come out next week.

Threat is also involved when teachers have unrealistic expectations for children, demanding or even cajoling (for subtlety can be full of threat) some kind of behavior which children, for whatever reason, are simply incapable of delivering:

> *Demanding:* Now boys and girls, you simply are not trying. You can get these sounds if you pay attention. So we'll go through them again, and if you still can't get them, we'll just stay at dismissal until we do.
> *Cajoling:* Of course you can sound out these words, Allen. You are a good, smart boy. You just have to try. Miss Brown wants to be proud of you, so come on, now there's a fine boy. What's this word again?

Thus threat comes in many guises, some of them overt and straightforward, some so subtle and roundabout that they are not even recognized by teachers as threat—moral sermons, for example, or less obviously the "Good Citizens" chart, which suggests patterns of behavior to which few healthy, active children could possibly conform with any degree of consistency, much as they might want to.

We also need to examine the threat induced in children when we encourage competition in learning, when we pit child against child in a race for extrinsic rewards—high marks, gold stars, extra privileges, positions in advanced groups, and the like:

> I like the way Sara is reading today—such expression! Why can't you all read that way, children?
>
> Well, Jack is tied with Audrey today on our book chart. Good work, Jack. And Audrey, you'd better get busy if you want your star.

It is true that many ill-advised adults, likening the school to business or industry, insist that since life is competitive, children should learn early to compete, and for rewards. But if schools are meant to enable people to fulfill their unique potentials, they cannot afford to neglect the "losers," who are necessarily always in the majority.

We are not saying that competition *per se* is bad. Where children or groups of children are well matched, where both have a fairly even chance of winning, competition can constitute a challenge and a stimulus. But minimally the use of competition in school must provide *everybody* with successful experiences some of the time. Unless this can be arranged, you as a teacher are deliberately planning to punish many of your pupils regardless of their efforts, and you can be certain that this punishment will prevent their continued efforts to perform the tasks you assign, all of which leads us to our second point, namely the disruptive effects of punishment.

PUNISHMENT

The purpose of punishment, says the punisher, is usually to prevent or change certain undesirable behaviors. We believe that it is often administered because of its use in creating threat. Yet its value as a suppresser and changer of responses is questionable, for it is obvious that punished behavior often recurs. Only in the presence of the punishing agent does punishment usually stick.

Punishment arouses strong, negative emotion which often becomes associated with the situation generally rather than with the action punished. The great trouble with this negative emotion is that it reduces the number and the range of meanings available to children in a learning situation (1, p. 12). When children are made unduly anxious, their attention shifts from the range of possible meanings available in a learning situation and is focused on the threat itself. There is less willingness to try new directions because of the fear of error. Whatever happens to be learned under threat is not learned for its own worth. It is learned just to reduce or eliminate the threat, if indeed it is learned at all. And what is often learned is a *set* to avoid the situation. This is clearly an unwanted concomitant of punishment.

Another difficulty with punishment is that it does not make clear just what is being punished or what should have been done instead of the punished act. Especially when honest mistakes are punished, is confusion likely to arise, since the error is not always seen in the midst of negative emotion. Actually, to eliminate an undesired response, extinction (non-reinforcement) rather than punishment is most effective:

	Punishment	*Extinction*
TEACHER:	Begin work.	Begin work.
PUPIL:	What do we do?	What do we do?
TEACHER:	It tells in the directions. Read them.	(Does not answer; looks at another pupil.)
PUPIL:	What do they mean?	Does it tell in the directions?
TEACHER:	Read them. Everybody else is.	(Walks past without comment.)
PUPIL (later):	Am I doing the right thing?	Reads directions.
TEACHER:	For heaven's sake! It tells you right there! Now be quiet and get to work!	(No comment.)
PUPIL:	(Whispering to his neighbor) Is this what we should do?	Continues working.

Extinction as a technique will not work if the pattern of fearful and anxious (dependent) behavior illustrated on the left has been repeated many times. But it may work well when such patterns are just starting, provided someone else does not get into the act. This leads us to another point about punishment: other pupils do get into the act, often. Pupils reinforce each other's behavior much of the time, just as they serve as imitative models for each other. In fact, they engage in considerable instruction, witting and unwitting.

Occasionally they tell each other things. They serve each other as models all the time, and, since the force of group approval is strong, they compete with teachers as the principal source of reinforcement.

So far it would appear that punishment *per se* is not very effective. We suspect that most teachers know this and that, in fact, they administer punishment not for its direct usefulness but to keep their threats real.

Most teachers rely on punishment because it "works." Threats *do* lead to action on the part of those threatened—action to escape, to avoid the punishment. Skinner puts it this way:

> The child at his desk, filling in his workbook, is behaving primarily to escape from the threat of a series of minor aversive events—the teacher's

displeasure, the criticism or ridicule of his classmates, an ignominious showing in a competition, low marks, a trip to the office "to be talked to" by the principal, or a word to the parent who may still resort to the birch rod. In this welter of aversive consequences, getting the right answer is in itself an insignificant event, any effect of which is lost amid the anxieties, the boredom, and the aggressions which are the inevitable by-products of aversive control (11, pp. 90-91).

To be sure, some children customarily are highly anxious about a great many things—things ordinarily beyond our control. Here we are concerned only about the additional anxiety imposed by the threats teachers make or build into their teaching operations.

In sum, we assert that threat creates a learning environment that works contrary to our purposes. It is a distractor from meaning, it focuses attention on escape and avoidance which generalizes readily to the whole school situation, it limits children's receptivity to new ideas, and it interferes with the growth of feelings of competence, adequacy, and worth. Yes, threat works! It galvanizes pupils into action, but it creates a set on the part of teachers and pupils alike that diminishes attention to meanings. In any area of learning this appears to be an undesirable outcome; in reading, we submit that it is disastrous.

Now perhaps you are thinking, "But I do respect children and do want to protect their integrity and help them develop self-esteem and positive feelings toward school and learning. And I do not believe in threats of punishment or competition to secure obedience and effort. Yet what is the alternative? How am I to reduce threat when much of school learning is precisely of the kind that pupils find dull and meaningless?"

Perhaps the best way to avoid the necessity for threat (or at least to reduce it) is to strive constantly to provide learning experiences that are meaningful to children because they are perceived as useful. Children are always responsive to situations that hold meanings for them, that excite their curiosities. But they are never genuinely responsive to situations that do not. The more useful reading can be made in solving problems, securing needed information, satisfying curiosities, the more children will seek reading:

> Here is a story you might like to look over and read aloud to use tomorrow . . .
>
> I think you will find what you are looking for in this book . . .
>
> See if your group would like to dramatize this story. Perhaps after you have looked it over, you could take the group into the workroom and tell them . . .

The problems approach is generally useful for investing an activity with meaning. Because problems usually have novel elements that excite attention and offer a challenge, and because children share in planning procedures and have a stake in outcomes, problems tend to enlist the energies of children, and the need for threat disappears or is materially reduced:

> While her fifth-graders finish writing up their report of a science experiment, Miss Jackson stands at her desk turning a pair of bar magnets over and over in her fingers. After a bit, a child looks up and asks what she is doing.
>
> MISS JACKSON: Have you finished, Sandy? . . .
> Well, if you must know, these magnets are not marked, so I'm figuring out which pole is which.
>
> SANDY: That's easy, Miss Jackson. Just put them together, and if they stick, one is north and the other south!
>
> MISS JACKSON: So you think it's that easy? All right, they're sticking together. So which pole is which?
>
> SANDY (points): This one is north and this one is south . . .
>
> MISS JACKSON: Are you sure?
>
> ARLENE: Oh, I see!
> (Other children call out, "So do I!" and begin waving hands.)
>
> MISS JACKSON: What do you see, Arlene?
>
> ARLENE: Well, it could be either way (explains the problem).
>
> MISS JACKSON: Right. Do you agree, Sandy? (Sandy agrees.) So, what do we do? One at a time, please! Robert?
>
> ROBERT: Well, you could . . . (At this point, Miss Jackson asks a pupil to write suggestions on the chalkboard.)
>
> A few minutes of discussion produce the following:
>
> 1. Float one magnet on a cork; north will swing to the north pole.
> 2. Tie the magnets in the middle with strings, and they will swing like a compass needle. Then you can tell.
> 3. Get a compass and point each magnet at it; the compass needle will tell which is which.
> 4. Look in the encyclopedia for help.
>
> Miss Jackson now selects two volunteers to check out each of the four suggestions and gives the children ten minutes for their research. The rest of her pupils continue work on their reports.

This example may arouse the comment that there isn't time for such "opportunistic" approaches and that they rarely coincide with the planned curriculum. But we believe that if you are not quick at shifting academic gears and at trying new approaches when a particular one breaks down, if you are not willing on occasion to postpone an experience or give it up entirely because it is dear to your heart and is called for by the guidebook, then what you are doing is allowing *your* concerns, feelings, and wishes to become central. When children are merely conforming to the wishes of the teacher, they become dependent on the teacher for reinforcement and direction. Such things as meaning, interest, and curiosity do not direct the pupils' learning behavior. We believe that many teachers actually like this dependency and use threat to encourage it, which leads us to our final point.

DEPENDENCE ON AUTHORITY

Strong dependency on others, like many other forms of behavior, is not bad in and of itself. It is bad because dependence is detrimental to the emotional and intellectual growth of children. It tends to stifle the very things that produce emotional and educational growth: the drive to know, curiosity, creative activity—motivation, if you will. Of course it may not stifle some kinds of growth. Dependent children *do* "get their lessons." They memorize what we want them to memorize, they compute by rote, and they imitate various kinds of behavior. But they rarely feel free to venture into the kinds of activities that help develop the rational powers: inquiry, analysis, synthesis. They rarely feel free to engage in the kinds of activities that tend to develop the capacity we most seek to develop in our schools: the capacity to *think,* which is the capacity to *learn,* which is the power of *solving problems.*

In this connection we recall Dewey's insistent dictum: if a child is to learn to think, he must go through the experience of:

> . . . wrestling with the conditions of the problem at first hand, seeking and finding his own way out. . . . If he cannot devise his own solutions (not of course in isolation, but in correspondence with the teacher and other pupils) and find his own way out he will not learn (4, p. 183).

When we unduly restrict the emotional and intellectual activities of children, we obviously limit their freedom to "wrestle with the conditions of the problem." Children thus restricted tend to become unable or afraid to question, to explore, to discover, to experiment. They soon lose initiative, become submissive and then dependent on authority for direction and support.

If we are to learn to solve problems, we need most of all to be unafraid to take chances, and this means that we must be unafraid of making mistakes. No one who works through any but the most elementary intellectual (or mechanical) problem ever proceeds unerringly to its solution. There is always trial and error, covert or overt. Thus to err is not simply human. It is an integral part of the problem-solving process and should therefore be recognized and accepted for what it is.

> The fully functioning personality, having accepted the ongoing nature of life and the dynamics of change, *sees the values of mistakes.* He knows he will be treading new paths at all times, and that, therefore, he cannot always be right . . . [He] will not only see that mistakes are inevitable in constantly breaking new ground, but will come to realize that these unprofitable paths show the way to better ones. Thus a mistake, which no one would make if he could foresee it, can be profitable (7, p. 19).

But too many teachers fail to recognize the inevitability (and useful-ness) of error in learning. They are disturbed by its presence and tend, subtly or openly, to punish it. They may become sarcastic, or play one child against another, or stop children from pushing ahead in a "chancy" line of reasoning or performing. They tend to develop passive or active distaste for mistake-makers. And because most children are highly anxious to please adults, to have them on their side, they tend to rely more and more on adult direction, adult ways of saying and doing things. They, too, become addicted to the avoidance of error, addicted to the "right" response. In this way self-reliance is reduced or destroyed and dependency takes its place.

If your relationships to your pupils are to promote learning in reading, they must be of the kind that set children free to ask questions and propose answers without fear of rejection, free to speculate about the reasons for things, free to share in planning possible approaches to prob-lems, free to manipulate, to explore, to experiment, to test out—and to make mistakes in the process.

When you visit a classoom in which such wholesome relationships exist, you simply do not hear such things as:

> How on earth did you get that answer? You can tell just by looking that. . . . Well, you can just start over again, and this time get it right!

> All right, let's stop guessing. You are getting way off the track, as anybody with half an eye could see . . .

Rather, one hears:

> You have 27 for your answer? Some of us got 26, but we could be wrong. Let's go over it together. You show me what you did, and I'll show you how I arrived at 26. Ted, would you and Nell check over your problem to make sure the answer *is* 26?

> I think some of you are just guessing now. By the way, what *is* a guess? Well, that's true. Let me ask you a question. I have a picture of something in my desk. What is it?

> *Pupils:* A horse! (a girl, a house, a farm, an airplane, a satellite . . .)

> Are you guessing? Why? Now suppose I tell you I have something in my pocketbook . . .

> *Pupils:* A lipstick! A wallet! Car keys!

> Car keys, right! Now are you doing the *same* kind of guessing? Why not?

You have probably noticed that all of our little classroom episodes involve teachers talking to children. We have presented them in this fashion to make our points crystal clear. However, we do not consider that teacher-talk is the essence of good instruction. As a matter of fact, when you talk, often you are actually interfering with pupil learning!

It is much better when pupils work with materials in ways planned previously or, even better, when they work through their own ideas if relevant to the solution of their problem.

Summing Up

The points we made at the beginning of this chapter may be used to summarize our concern about giving children the freedom to learn, thus giving you what we hope is a clear example of the relevance of these points to reading and meaning.

Threat focuses attention on the teacher's purpose, but remember our first point:

Teachers cannot learn for their pupils; it is the actions of pupils that determine what they learn.

Think of your own actions (including your thoughts) when you are threatened or have just been punished. What is your set? Remember our second point:

What a pupil does depends on his set.

And set depends on the features of the situation that the pupil sees as relevant:

What a pupil sees as relevant depends on the meanings he brings to and derives from the learning materials.

If the materials are always associated with fear and unpleasantness, what sort of meanings are brought to them?

When you threaten and punish a pupil, you are *telling* him he is not good and, maybe, that you don't like him. You are *showing* him that you can make him do things and can push him around. And you are creating automatic *reinforcement* for all his efforts at escape and avoidance of the learning situation (your classroom). Remember that:

Reinforcement is a central part of the learning process.

And since threat seems to work, *you* are being reinforced in its use. Thus each time you use threat you are increasing the chances that you will threaten or punish some more.

Teaching is complicated, and:

Repetition or practice is at the heart of learning any complicated material or skill that consists of many parts.

And so you are learning to be a threatener and punisher. As you practice this in an ever-increasing variety and number of ways, the behavior becomes more and more representative of your teaching style, your teaching ability:

After long practice, skills tend to coalesce in organized patterns or abilities that then become difficult to change.

As an added note, we should say that while we have been talking mostly about the pupils, you can see that we are interested in teachers too. We like teachers, we want pupils to like teachers, we want pupils to like school and learning, and we want teachers to like them too!

Because of the nature of learning and instruction, the use of threat and punishment as the major device for controlling pupil activity creates a trap for teachers that leads away from a concern for meaning; yet those same principles demand that a concern for meaning be at the forefront of any effort to teach reading. Now we must acknowledge again, these devices work. We must go further: if not used too often, if the threat is kept mild, if the punishment is almost like a natural consequence, these devices are not too harmful. We in fact use them ourselves. As we examine the book to this point, this chapter, this section, we realize that we ourselves have made use of threat. For example, we've hinted darkly that "Your pupils won't like you." We apologize: *nostra culpa!* And we rationalize: our threats were mild, they were not frequent, we did not punish (because we could not), and therefore any consequences are almost natural.

Let us turn to more positive things. You are interested in practical problems, and your interests (in your role as our students) take precedence over ours. In the next chapter we try to illustrate what we have been talking about in this book by way of a series of classroom vignettes.

Bibliography

1. Combs, Arthur W., "Personality Theory and Its Implications for Curriculum Development," in *Learning More About Learning,* Papers and Reports for the Third A.S.C.D. Research Institute, ed. Alexander Frazier. Washington, D.C.: The National Education Association, 1959.

2. ————, "Seeing Is Believing." *Educational Leadership* 16 (1): 22-23; October 1958.

3. Darrow, Helen Fisher, and Virgil M. Howes, *Approaches to Individualized Reading.* New York: Appleton-Century-Crofts, 1960.

4. Dewey, John, *Democracy and Education.* New York: The Macmillan Company, 1916.

5. Fries, Charles, *Linguistics and Reading.* New York: Holt, Rinehart & Winston, Inc., 1963.

6. Green, Donald Ross, *Educational Psychology.* Englewood Cliffs, N.J.: Prentice-Hall, 1964.

7. Kelley, Earl C., "The Fully Functioning Self." *Perceiving, Behaving, Becoming: A New Focus for Education.* 1962 Yearbook, Arthur W. Combs, chairman. Washington, D.C.: Association for Supervision and Curriculum Development, NEA, 1962.

8. Lazar, May, ed., *A Practical Guide to Individualized Reading,* Publication No. 40. New York: Bureau of Educational Research, Board of Education, City of New York, 1960.

9. McCandless, Boyd R., *Children: Behavior and Development* (2nd ed.). New York: Holt, Rinehart & Winston, Inc., 1967.

10. Maslow, A. H., *Motivation and Personality.* New York: Harper & Row, Publishers, 1954.

11. Skinner, B. F., "The Science of Learning and the Art of Teaching," *Harvard Educational Review,* Vol. 24, No. 2, Spring 1954.

12. Stone, L. Joseph, and Joseph Church, *Childhood and Adolescence.* New York: Random House, Inc., 1957.

13. Tilton, J. W., *An Educational Psychology of Learning.* New York: The Macmillan Company, 1951.

14. Veatch, Jeannette, *Individualizing Your Reading Program.* New York: G. P. Putnam's Sons, 1959.

15. Wheat, Harry G., *Foundations of School Learning.* New York: Alfred A. Knopf, Inc., 1955.

CHAPTER VI

CLASSROOM VIGNETTES: MEANING, LANGUAGE, AND LEARNING IN READING

Having discussed meaning, language, and learning as they function in the reading process, we now offer a series of episodes to illustrate how all of these can and do work together in the classroom. Accompanying each episode are commentary—our interpretation of the action—and suggestions for alternative procedures, if in our opinion these are warranted.

Most of our vignettes are drawn from life; only the names have been changed to protect the innocent—or the guilty, as the case may be. A few episodes are the products of our own thinking about how instruction might proceed when teachers are knowledgeable, or not knowledgeable, about the roles of meaning, language, and learning in reading.

We hope that these descriptions will illuminate those aspects of the reading process we have discussed and will provide useful notions for planning and carrying out more effective reading experiences in classroom and home.

It might be interesting for you to mask our comments until you have made your own analysis of each vignette. In this way, you will be checking how well you have *read* what we have written about reading for meaning!

1.

In her second grade, Miss Blair has given each child in Jack's group two 4 x 6 cards. One

We think Miss Blair's plan to help her pupils differentiate the bears the letters *st* in manuscript, and the other, *str*. She has printed on large cards a number of words, all of which are within the "hearing-meaning" vocabulary of her pupils:

string	stone
straw	steeple
strap	steps
street	stick
strawberry	stocking
strip	stove

She places each card one at a time on the chalkboard tray, at the same time pronouncing the word, and displaying either the object represented by the word (as a piece of string) or an unambiguous picture of the object. As she does so, children repeat the word and hold up the card bearing what they believe to be the appropriate consonant combination.

When the blends are pretty well learned, Miss Blair arranges for a team contest, each team retaining the word cards that team members correctly pronounce.

two consonant blends is good because:

1. Meanings are reinforced by relating words to their referents (the objects they represent).
2. Miss Blair forces discrimination between the blends.
3. Each child is directly involved in the task; each is required to make successive discriminations.
4. Miss Blair can immediately correct errors made by any child.

On the other hand, Miss Blair has unwittingly provided irrelevant cues by including certain words in her two lists: *sto* has the o cue which no *str* word has, while *str* has a cues lacking in the *st* words. She might well have included *strong* in the first list and *star* in the second.

Miss Blair did well not to have the words used in sentences at this point. To do so, since *meanings* are not a problem, would have introduced an irrelevancy into the task situation. Later on, for another experience, she might follow up by distributing the word cards and having pupils devise sentences using the words.

As for the competition introduced by the game, Miss Blair waited until the blends were pretty well learned, so that she was confident that all could share in their team's success as each team accumulated word cards. Even the losers would have company.

2.

Mrs. Levy notes that she and her sixth-graders have ten minutes before lunch.

MRS. LEVY: Yes, we can play the IF game. Do you remember how it goes?

The teacher's questions keep the children's attention focused on *meanings*. Also, she can get immediate clues about what chil-

NANCY: Well, we say something beginning with IF, like, if . . .

JACK: If I get hungry . . .

NANCY: Then I eat!

MRS. LEVY: Is that right? Does it *follow?*

CHILDREN: Yes!

MRS. LEVY: How do you know it's right, it follows?

BILL: Because it makes sense. It isn't funny.

MRS. LEVY: Makes sense? Isn't funny?

BILL: Well, we do eat when we are hungry. That isn't funny. It makes sense. That's what you *do!*

MRS. LEVY: Then what's an IF that doesn't make sense, that's funny?

MARK: If I get hungry, then . . . then I fly a kite! (Children laugh) See? It's funny.

MRS. LEVY: OK. Now what about *because?*

JACK: You can say it with because, too. Like, *Because* I am hungry, I eat. You have to use because. It's part of the game.

MRS. LEVY: Fine. Sam, here's your list, and here's yours, Ellen. Who starts?

SAM: My team. Begin with Ellen. Ellen, if I feel sleepy . . .

ELLEN: I go to bed.

SAM: Nope. Carol?

CAROL: *Then* I go to bed!

SAM: All right. Now what else?

CAROL: *Because* I am sleepy, I go to bed.

SAM: OK. Bob, if I spill my milk . . .

dren do and do not understand with respect to cause and effect statements.

Note that the game deals with a major aspect of language: the logical statement. This sort of language-logic exercise is part of reading instruction. It may, of course, be thought of by the teacher as part of something else, such as language arts or English or even mathematics. But no reading program is complete without the kind of language experience here transcribed. The reading teacher must make sure it is included.

This experience contributes to the development of a learning set which will enable pupils to deal more effectively with cause and effect relationships found in written forms.

3.

Mrs. Cope's third-grade group is having trouble with the spelling and meaning of some of the words in the pledge to the flag.

MRS. COPE: Children, put down your books. We need to get some of the words right in the pledge to the flag. Your spelling has been very poor. Watch me, please (writes on the chalkboard):

a-l-l-e-g-i-a-n-c-e
i-n-d-i-v-i-s-i-b-l-e
l-i-b-e-r-t-y
j-u-s-t-i-c-e

Spell with me, all together now! A-l-l-e-g-i-a-n-c-e. Fine. Once again. A-l-l-e-g-i-a-n-c-e.

The teacher is concerned with both meanings and spelling, and has realized by listening to the pupils that many of the words in the pledge are a mystery to them. So far, so good.

But her approach to spelling improvement leaves much to be desired, and if she thinks (as she clearly does) that pronouncing words somehow imparts their meanings, she is a victim of the false notion that words have intrinsic meanings!

Mrs. Cope would do much bet-

Good. Now let's say it together: *allegiance*. Once again: *allegiance*. Good. Now we know what it means, don't we?

Now all together: i-n-d-i-v-i-s-i-b-l-e. Say it: *indivisible*. Spell it together once more. . . .

ter to help her young charges compose what they conceive to be a patriotic pledge and commit it to memory, until such time as she is able to make the "Pledge" words meaningful by somehow relating them to the experiences of the pupils. The words *indivisible* and *liberty* might not be too difficult, but how about *allegiance* and *justice*?

Finally, Mrs. Cope would do well to help her pupils realize that the "Pledge" is a kind of ritual and that *reciting* it is not the same as *living* its message.

4.

Mrs. Buck often writes such things as the following on the chalkboard for her third-graders:

pencil	flag
book	picture
yellow	dress
mother	grr-r-r-r
love	

MRS. BUCK: (Holds up a pencil.) Children, what is this?

CHILDREN: A pencil!

MRS. BUCK: (Points to the pencil.) This is a pencil. (Points to the word *pencil*.) Then what is this?

DEBBIE: That's *pencil*, too!

MRS. BUCK: But which is the real thing?

CHILDREN: What's in your hand!

GRACE: In your hand! That's a pencil!

MRS. BUCK: (Points to the word *pencil*.) Then what is this?

CHILDREN: The word! The word!

MRS. BUCK: The word *what*?

LINDA: The *word* pencil. It isn't a real pencil at all!

MRS. BUCK: All right. (Holds up small flag.) What's this?

CHILDREN: A flag. American flag!

MRS. BUCK: (Points to word *flag*.) And this?

CHILDREN: The *word* flag!

This give and take helps children make distinctions not only between words and things, but also between "concrete" words such as *table* and *chair*, and abstract concepts such as *love*.

Note that Mrs. Buck doesn't *tell* children; she guides their thinking by skillful questioning and reinforces the appropriate responses. Not all pupils will be thinking along with the teacher, of course, since the slower ones will be "told the answer" by the quicker ones. To fully realize this technique, Mrs. Buck would need to question children individually.

Note also that words may sometimes be treated as things in themselves, as when we study the structure of language.

As children through these and other kinds of "language games" grow more sophisticated, Mrs. Buck hopes that they will be helped to analyze more complex linguistic traps such as:

Pigs are rightly named because they are so dirty.

MRS. BUCK: (Still pointing to the word.) So this isn't a flag?

ARTHUR: No, no, Mrs. Buck! That's the *word* flag.

MRS. BUCK: Arthur, if you asked me for a flag, which should I give you? This? (Points to the word *flag*.)

ARTHUR: No! Give me this flag (comes up and takes flag).

MRS. BUCK: Yes, but . . . what about words?

MARTIN: Well, they're things, I guess. But not the real things!

MRS. BUCK: Are words like desks?

MARTIN: No.

MRS. BUCK: Are words like chairs? Can you sit on them?

CHILDREN: No! No!

MRS. BUCK: Then what are words?

ALICE: Words point to things—like chairs.

MRS. BUCK: Words point . . . ?

ALICE: They are *instead of* chairs and things . . .

MRS. BUCK: They *stand for* things?

MARTIN: Yes. They *stand* for things!

MRS. BUCK: So when I *say* "church," there's no church?

CALEB: No. Only the word.

MRS. BUCK: (Points to *love*.) What's this?

CHILDREN: Love.

MRS. BUCK: Can I put love in the desk drawer?

CHILDREN: No!

MRS. BUCK: Can I hold up some love or wash it?

CHILDREN: No!

MRS. BUCK: Then there is no *love* in the room?

MARGARET: Well, you love us, Mrs. Buck!

MRS. BUCK: But I can't hold any up, or wash it out?

CHILDREN: No!

MRS. BUCK: But I can write the word that *stands for* love, for how I feel about you children?

CHILDREN: Yes!

The Divine is rightly named.

She may later on help pupils see that the "stand for" notion does not apply to all words (such as *for, because,* and the like) but for now, she finds the procedure a useful one at the pupils' stage of concept development.

P.S. Mrs. Buck was called to the office just as she started to work with *grr-r-r-r.* How would you like to finish the lesson with the children while she is gone?

5.

Mr. Hope and his sixth-grade pupils are discussing the games to be played at recess.

JACK: Why is Mr. Sommers called a *coach?* He doesn't have any wheels! (General laughter.)

The teacher takes immediate steps to capitalize on pupils' interests to enlarge their understandings of the concept of *coach.*

MR. HOPE: Fine question! Can anyone help us out?

ARNOLD: A coach is a wagon, too.

MR. HOPE: Yes, and it means to teach, doesn't it? Jack, how's about getting the dictionary and looking it up for us? In the meantime— back at the desk—Susan, will you get the manila folder from the front of the big cabinet? Right there. Thanks. Jack?

JACK: Coach. A large, closed carriage with seats inside and often on top. A passenger railroad car. A closed automobile. . . . To teach, train.

MR. HOPE: Thanks, Jack. (Opens folder and displays colored photographs—first, a stagecoach.) Is this a coach? How about this? (English coach-and-four.) And this? (An airliner.) And this one? (A rickshaw.) Now if your mother and dad wanted to know what a coach is, could you tell them? How are these all alike?

WILMA: They carry people!

MR. HOPE: O.K.

MABEL: The dictionary said a coach is a teacher, too. So Mr. Sommers *is* a coach, because he teaches the boys how to play basketball.

MR. HOPE: Right. How do you suppose the word coach came to mean two such different things—a vehicle and a teacher?

Further, the teacher is reinforcing efforts at getting meaning by supporting Jack's question and by involving Jack in the solution of the problem.

His picture file is second best only to having the real vehicles at hand.

Finally, the teacher helps pupils focus on the relevant aspect of the discussion by asking how the vehicles are all alike.

By his final question Mr. Hope might hope to (check which):

a. Confuse the pupils in order to stimulate thought.
b. Help them see the arbitrary nature of language.
c. Arouse student interest In word origins.

6.

In Miss Pine's fourth grade, pupils are listening to a classmate reading a story he has found and likes.

ALBERT: Jack tasted the pudding and made a grim . . . a grim-sase. Made a grimsase.

MISS PINE: Is it grimsase?

SALLY: No, it's *grim-mass*.

MISS PINE: Well, that's a good try. How would you pronounce *a-c-e?*

CHILDREN: Ace!

MISS PINE: Right. Ace. What's the word, Audrey?

AUDREY: Grim-mace. Grimace.

MISS PINE: Right. Do you know what a grimace is? The story says that Jack made a grimace.

NAN: A face!

MISS PINE: Any other ideas? Well, that's right.

This we deem a useful procedure for the following reasons:

a. The teacher makes use of similarity and contrast to develop and extend meaning.
b. She provides a concrete referent for a new word.
c. She allows each child to "experience" the new word by acting it out.

Note that Miss Pine passed up the opportunity to poke fun at Albert for his mispronunciation. Some teachers might not have missed the chance!

A face. Do you know what *kind* of face Jack made? A grin? A frown? We have some disagreement. Watch me and I'll try to grimace for you—*make* a grimace. (Twists face into a wry smile-frown of disapproval.)

CHILDREN: Oh, Miss Pine, you're so funny!

MISS PINE: Now watch (smiles). Now watch (frowns).

CHILDREN: That's a smile. That's a frown.

MISS PINE: Now my grimace (twists face again).

CHILDREN: Yes, yes, that's a grimace. Do it again!

MISS PINE: Suppose we all do it. Bruce, you begin.

JOE: I know, I know! Miss Pine, let's each do something and the others guess what it is. You can smile or frown or grimace, and we'll guess.

MISS PINE: A fine idea. Do you want to begin, Bruce?

7.

Mrs. Jones' third grade is reading from their social studies textbook.

MRS. JONES: What part did you like as far as you have read?

JOAN: I like the part that tells how bananas grow. I never knew that before.

MRS. JONES: Would you like to read it to us?

JOAN: 'There are many banana plantations in the warm lands. Some have many hundreds of trees. The fruit does not grow the way we see it in the store. As the picture shows, it grows up instead of down. For this reason, the banana is sometimes called the "upside down" fruit.'

MRS. JONES: Do you think this is a good name for the banana, boys and girls?

CHILDREN: Yes!

MRS. JONES: Very good. George, what part did you like?

Mrs. Jones accomplishes several worthwhile things by having pupils select and read favorite parts: pupils' attention is focussed on major points made by the selection; the relevance of favorite parts read can be discussed; pupils' comprehension of material can be checked without the formality of a test; pupils get the chance to practice oral reading.

However, Mrs. Jones misses the opportunity to enlarge pupils' understanding of spatial relationships by failing to pick up the notion of the banana as an "upside down" fruit. The dialogue might better have gone something like this:

Mrs. Jones: Do you think that is a good name for the banana, Joan?

Joan: I guess so. It grows upside down!

Mrs. Jones: Does the banana really grow upside down?

Joan: Well . . .

Mrs. Jones: Do flowers grow upside down?

Children: No!

Mrs. Jones: How do they grow?

Joan: They grow rightside up. They grow *up*.

Mrs. Jones: They grow up—toward the sky?

Joan: Yes, they grow up—up toward the sky.

Mrs. Jones: Do you think nature grows things upside down?

Children: No! Things grow up.

Mrs. Jones: Then why "upside down" fruit?

Joan: Well, it grows one way, and in the store it hangs the other way.

Mrs. Jones: What is up? Down? Is there any up In space? On the moon, where is up?

8.

Miss Grey has set up three basal reader groups in her first grade: Group A (slow), Group B (average), and Group C (fast). Each group reads for about 30 minutes each morning under Miss Grey's guidance. Today, she is working with the "slow" group. The pupils are sitting with their readers in a small semicircle. Groups B and C are copying on lined paper the sentences (paraphrases of children's statements) that Miss Grey has printed on the chalkboard:

> Today is Tuesday.
> It is a nice day.
> The sun is shining.
> We go to the zoo tomorrow.

MISS GREY: Open your books to page 23. That's two-three. Look, I'll write it on the board. So . . . ! Lee, look at the board. The number is not on my nose. Find the page. Do you all have it? Jack, help Alice find the page. All ready? (A child from Group B approaches Miss Grey and starts to ask a question.) Back to your seat. We don't interrupt while I'm busy!

Slap!

Bop!

All right. Is everyone on page 23? Joan, find the page for Carol. All right. What's the name of the story? Wait, wait! One at a time! (Turns to the children at their desks.) What's all the talking? Ned and Billy! Back to your seats right now. I don't want to speak to you again!

All right, Joan. You read the first page for us. (Joan is unable to pronounce the first word.)

Once, once!

JOAN: Once a . . .

MISS GREY: Once *upon* . . .

JOAN: Once upon a . . .

MISS GREY: Time.

JOAN: Time. Once upon a time . . .

MISS GREY: There. Start again.

JOAN: Once upon a time there was a . . .

MISS GREY: Father.

JOAN: Father buh . . . buh . . .

MISS GREY: Now what's the title of the story? What animal are we reading about?

CHILDREN: Bear! Bear!

MISS GREY: Who's asking you? I'm talking to Joan. Are you Joan? You? You? Then be quiet.

JOAN: Bear.

MISS GREY: Start from the beginning, and read with expression, like you know what you are reading.

JOAN: What's this word?

MISS GREY: Once, once, once!

JOAN: Once up . . . upon a time . . . th-th-th . . .

MISS GREY: There! Let Carol read. Start from the beginning.

Smack!

Pow!

Thud!

Kaboom! Now they are *all* dead. What do you think?

9.

In the second grade, Miss Posner's pupils are writing original "scary" stories to commemorate Halloween.

MRS. POSNER: Here are the words you told me you want to use. They are all spelled out on the board for you. Do you have any others?

BECKY: We don't have *goblin*.

MRS. POSNER: That's right. Will you spell it for

Mrs. Posner is helping children develop (express) a vocabulary beyond that of the standard reader. She provides the way to bring out children's "hearing-meaning" vocabulary which is much more extensive than that of primary readers.

us? Fine. Are there any others? Very well, how many words do we have now?

CHILDREN: Fifteen!

MRS. POSNER: Are you sure?

JANICE: Yes! Fifteen!

MRS. POSNER: If I put them in groups of *five*, how many groups would I have?

ROBERT: Four!

JANICE: No, no! Three. Three fives make fifteen!

MRS. POSNER: Robert, would you come to the board and frame each group of five for us? There! We *do* have three groups, don't we? Thank you.

Now, I would like those who suggested words to come to the board and point to them, and pronounce them for us . . .

Thank you all. Perhaps it would help if we put together the words beginning with the same sound. You tell me, and I'll arrange them over here. All right . . . *pumpkin* and *pickle*. Do they go together? *Ghost, goblin, gallop*. Do they? Any more? Fine; now let's look for a moment at *ghost* . . .

Mrs. Posner also seizes the opportunity to refresh the children's arithmetic abilities.

Mrs. Posner made sure that any negative effects from Robert's arithmetic goof are dissipated by allowing him to display his competence promptly.

Finally, the phonic exercise grows naturally out of a meaningful experience with words; it is "in context," so to speak.

10.

In his fifth grade, Mr. Lyle has devised the following experience. He has written on the chalkboard:

Bill Martin is wearing a yellow sport shirt.
Sara Parsons is wearing a blue dress.
Mr. Lyle wears glasses.
Exams are fun.

The pupils react with vigor:

PUPILS: No! No! We don't like exams!

MR. LYLE: O.K., O.K., so you don't like exams! Do you notice anything about these sentences?

HARRY: Sure! The first three tell about what somebody is wearing. Where do exams fit in?

MR. LYLE: You think it's out of place?

TOM: Well, sure! What have exams to do with what you're wearing?

MR. LYLE: Not much, I suppose. But what about these four sentences? Are they true?

GRACE: The first three are. Bill and Sara *are*

To help pupils distinguish between statements that admit of proof and statements that do not, Mr. Lyle has wisely used as his first material the obvious and familiar (clothing *vs.* exams), then moved on to the less familiar syllogism which is a logical scheme of a formal argument, involving deductive reasoning. Here again, the teacher has presented first a syllogism involving familiar "content," baseball, then moved on to the abstraction involving A, B, and C.

This illustrative experience points up the one-to-one relationship between reading and reasoning: those who cannot reason to a valid conclusion are not *reading* the material, no matter wearing what you say. And you wear glasses.

HARRY: I see, I see! You can *see* what the kids are wearing, but how can you *see* exams are fun when they aren't!

CHERYL: Oh, I don't know. I don't mind exams!

CHILDREN: (good-naturedly) Oh, *you!*

MR. LYLE: All right, what kinds of statements do we have here?

ENID: Well, we have three statements true, and one that's . . . well, that's . . .

GRACE: Not true—not for me, anyway!

MR. LYLE: Could we say that the first three are statements of fact?

CHILDREN: Yes!

MR. LYLE: And could we say the last is a statement of opinion, depending upon who said it?

CHILDREN: Yes!

MR. LYLE: So the truth of the last statement depends on what?

CHILDREN: Who says it!

HARRY: Yeah, Cheryl likes exams! It's true for her. Not for me, boy!

MR. LYLE: Now we're getting somewhere. Who would like to check out these? Alex?

> America is the greatest land of all.
> Bears hibernate in winter.
> Japanese are sneaky people.
> School is a good place to be.
> My desk is 54 inches long.

ALEX: Well, America . . . hmmm. That's true. That's a statement of fact, I mean.

GEORGE: Ha! How about the Russians? Do *they* think America is the greatest land of all?

BILL: Yeah, how about the French? And the Germans? And . . .

MR. LYLE: Then who does?

CHILDREN: *We* do!

MR. LYLE: Go ahead, Alex.

ALEX: Well, bears do hibernate in winter. That's a fact. Japanese . . . well, *they* don't think so!

MR. LYLE: If they don't think so, does this make the statement a matter of opinion?

GEORGE: How would you *prove* it?

ALEX: That's opinion. How can *all* Japanese be sneaky?

MR. LYLE: Doing fine! Now how about these:

> The Mets won the league pennant!
> Kranepool is the first baseman.

how well they can call the words.

Because arguments of all kinds are often cast in syllogistic form, and because many are false (hence misleading), we think it valuable for pupils to learn to analyze them, to detect illogic where it exists. With respect to Mr. Lyle's procedure, we approve because (pick the answer):

a. There is movement from the concrete and familiar to the abstract, hence unfamiliar.

b. He doesn't confuse the pupils by combining false and true syllogisms.

c. Students should understand the importance of getting at the truth.

Therefore he is the best first baseman in the league.

No communist goes to church.
Mr. X doesn't go to church.
Therefore he's a communist.

All B's are A.
All C's are B.
Therefore all C's are A.

11.

Miss Hahn enacts little dramas for her second-grade pupils who then orally describe what she has done. Today, she has gone into the hall and reentered, wearing a bright red knitted cap. She goes to her desk, opens the top right drawer, lifts out a stuffed cat, strokes it gently several times, replaces it, removes her cap, rings a small bell on her desk, and goes back into the hall. She returns.

MISS HAHN: Who would like to tell the story? Whose turn is it? Nell?

NELL: You went in the hall and then you came back, and you patted the kitty and you rang the bell and you went out.

GRADY: You forgot, you forgot!

MISS HAHN: What, Grady?

GRADY: You took off your hat!

MISS HAHN: Would you like to try again, Nell?

SUSAN: And she didn't say *first* . . .

NELL: *First* you came in the room. Then you took out the kitty. Then you petted it. Then you put it back. Then . . . then . . . then you took off your cap. Then you rang the bell. Then you went out.

MISS HAHN: Where is the kitty?

CHILDREN: In the desk!

MISS HAHN: We do start with *first*. Why do we start with *first?*

PETER: Because that's how it *starts.*

MISS HAHN: Nell also said then. Is there another word which means *then?*

GRADY: Next! Next!

MISS HAHN: Yes. First, then, next . . . and so on. Shall we write our story on the board, just as it happened?

Miss Hahn employs a catchy situation to create a set for observing the sequence of events. Having pupils put events in sequence provides practice in one of the major intellectual skills in reading: taking ideas in order.

Miss Hahn is helping children develop precise verbal expression. She begins with oral expression and then moves to its written counterpart—which is the natural progression: "Reading is speech wrote down."

The follow up of writing the story should increase set, or general expectation that written materials exhibit ideas in order, just as spoken language does.

On another day, Miss Hahn might plan with two or three pupils to stage a similar "drama" for the class. This would add another dimension reinforcing the general notion and would provide children with the chance for active involvement.

12.

Mrs. Brown has asked third-grade Sally to write some sentences on the board.

MRS. BROWN: Sally has written her sentences beautifully, hasn't she, children? Sally, you do write *such* a pretty hand! Children, do you suppose you could write just as nicely as Sally when you come to the board?

JANE: Oh, Mrs. Brown! Sally forgot to put a dot over the *i*.

MRS. BROWN: Nancy, can you make it right for Sally? Thank you. Do you see anything else, children?

PENNY: And a dot at the end.

MRS. BROWN: What do we call the dot at the end?

CHILDREN: A period!

MRS. BROWN: Yes. Very good. Sally, will you fix it for us? Now read it to us, George. Very good. Now what are the rules about the *i* and about the end of sentences?

CINDY: When you finish saying something, you put a period.

MRS. BROWN: Why?

PETE: Because that's the rule. You stop.

MRS. BROWN: How about the *i* rule?

DAVID: That's a rule, too. You always dot the *i*.

There appears to be a total lack of concern on the part of Mrs. Brown with the central notion: *meaning*. She has taken every opportunity to create a set that notions other than meaning are the important ones, i.e., the rules of punctuation, obeying authority without question. Mrs. Brown might well have proceeded in some such way as the following:

Walter: Oh, Mrs. Brown! Sally forgot to put a dot over the *i!*

Mrs. Brown: What difference? Why should she dot the *i?*

Children: That's the rule!

Mrs. Brown: Rule, of course. Why do we have such a rule?

Sally: Well, because the book says so.

Mrs. Brown: Well, that's true. But look! (Writes on board several words with undotted *i*'s which she shapes to resemble *e*'s.) Alice, can you read these to us?

Alice: Pen, mend, letter, led.

Mrs. Brown: No, no! I'm sorry. The words are pin, mind, litter, and lid.

Children: No! No! They are pen, mend . . .

Mrs. Brown: But I wrote them, so I know what they are!

George: But Mrs. Brown! They are *e*'s.

Mrs. Brown: Well, they may *look* like *e*'s. I wrote them in a hurry, but they are supposed to be *i*'s!

Children: Then put dots over them, so we'll know!

Mrs. Brown: All right! Great! (Dots the *e*'s with exaggerated dots.) Now can you read my words?

Children: Pin, mind, litter, lid!

Mrs. Brown: Fine! Now do you see anything else about Sally's sentence?

13.

In the fourth grade, pupils have just finished a story about a boy who fell heir to a neighbor's horse.

MRS. CHEN: Did everyone come to love old Champ?

MARK: Boy! Champ was a great horse!

MRS. CHEN: Mark, find the part that tells what everyone thought about Champ, will you please?

MARK: 'Daddy said, "Champ is a good horse!" and the Smith family echoed his words.'

MRS. CHEN: Did they all think Champ a good horse for the same reason? Carl?

CARL: Well, Liza liked Champ because he ate up all the old potato peelings!

MRS. CHEN: That made Champ a *good* horse?

CARL: Yes.

MRS. CHEN: All right. Where do you find that in the story? Yes, read it to us. (Carl reads.) Very good, now how about Mother Smith?

BESSIE: Because Champ stayed in the backyard where he belonged.

MRS. CHEN: How about Daddy Smith?

RAYMOND: Because Champ pulled the carriage all over town on Oldtimer's Day.

MRS. CHEN: Can you read that part for us, Ray?

RAYMOND: *Yes.* (Reading.) 'No horse in the world was prouder than old Champ as he pulled Daddy Smith up and down the streets of Ma . . . May . . . Mapleton. And no daddy was more proud than Daddy Smith!'

MRS. CHEN: Well, now, were their reasons all alike—for thinking Champ was a good horse, I mean?

CHILDREN: No!

RAYMOND: They all had different reasons!

MRS. CHEN: What does this tell us about the word *good?*

RALPH: It means different things . . .

MRS. CHEN: Yes, it seems to. Suppose . . . suppose I pointed to a person and said, 'He is *bad.*' What would you have to know?

RALPH: Well, we'd have to know *why.*

MRS. CHEN: You wouldn't know *why,* if I said, 'He is bad'?

BESSIE: Well, he isn't good!

MRS. CHEN: But you wouldn't know *why* he isn't good?

CARL: No . . .

Things (and people and animals and ideas) mean different things to different people, depending on their experiences with these things (and people and animals and ideas). Mrs. Chen is capitalizing on the situation in a simple story to help her pupils realize this important notion. She has developed understandings about the "meaning of meaning" and the variability of meaning which enable her to go beyond a mere story and help children unravel some of the mysteries of meaning.

Note, however, that after doing pretty well for a while, Mrs. Chen—after Bessie's last comment —falls into her own trap! She might better have picked up Bessie's comment by asking, "How do you know he isn't good?"

Also, Mrs. Chen repeatedly has pupils go to the book to substantiate their answers, thus creating a set for getting the intended meaning rather than imposing one's own preconceptions. This is part of the "art" of reading.

MRS. CHEN: Do you have to know *why* I think he is bad?

CARL: Well, *why* is he bad? . . .

14.

Mr. Payne often calls attention to strange "homemade" objects. He creates and exhibits odd-looking "tools" and painted abstractions, which pupils then talk about. Today he has displayed a paper toweling tube painted black and pierced by a slender metal bar.

MR. PAYNE: How about this?

DOUGLAS: It's a telescope!

SAMMY: It's a kal . . . kal . . .

MR. PAYNE: Kaleidoscope? (Writes the word on the board.)

SAMMY: Yes, kal-i-doscope!

DAISY: What's the nail for?

CHILDREN: It's not a telescope! They don't have nails in them!

AMY: Neither does a kaleidoscope.

MR. PAYNE: What is it called?

SAMMY: I don't know. What's it used for?

CHILDREN: To blow through? To look through? To hit with?

MR. PAYNE: It's not for anything. What shall we call it?

CARLENE: You can't call it anything, if it's not for anything!

MR. PAYNE: No? What did we do last week, with that . . .

CARLENE: I know, I know!

NELSON: Call it a black tube with a nail in it!

SAMMY: Aw, call it something you can say, like . . . like *blob!*

MR. PAYNE: Would *glabber* do just as well? How about *kerplop?*

SALLY: I like *glabber!*

MR. PAYNE: Why do we have to name it, anyway?

NELSON: It's shorter than saying "black tube with a nail in it."

MR. PAYNE: Well, suppose tomorrow you wanted to see it again.

SALLY: Then we say, "Where's the *glabber!*"

MR. PAYNE: Does it make any difference what we call it?

Mr. Payne's creations are attention-getting devices for helping pupils understand that verbal labels are arbitrary and that people and things and ideas may be called anything we like, so long as we agree on the label. Words are not things.

When Mr. Payne asks Nelson, "Why do we have to name it, anyway?" he is getting at what language can do for thinking, and how or why reading is communication.

Note that Mr. Payne takes a moment to spell out *kaleidoscope,* but fails to discuss or mention its function.

Mr. Payne might follow up such experiences as these by having pupils write descriptions of weird things which need "names."

Mr. Payne uses the quotation from Shakespeare to provide pupils with an additional chance to practice drawing the proper inference from a new context, which neatly summarizes the central point.

CHILDREN: No! No difference!

MR. PAYNE: Shakespeare . . .

CARLENE: He was a writer.

MR. PAYNE: Yes. He once wrote, 'A rose by any other name would smell as sweet.' Do you believe that?

CARLENE: Call a rose a glabber! (laughter)

MR. PAYNE: Would it smell as sweet?

15.

Mrs. Lyke's fifth-graders are reviewing their weekly spelling list. Specifically, they are studying certain ways of pluralizing nouns with *o* and *ium* endings.

MRS. LYKE: Take the first word, Jane.

JANE: Solo. Add *s*.

MRS. LYKE: Yes, what do you get?

JANE: Solos.

MRS. LYKE: Robert?

ROBERT: Motto. Add *s*.

MRS. LYKE: Wrong. Jack?

JACK: Add *es*.

MRS. LYKE: Right. What's the plural, Robert?

ROBERT: Mottoes.

MRS. LYKE: Spell it.

ROBERT: M-o-t-t-o-e-s.

MRS. LYKE: Don't forget that. Elaine?

ELAINE: Gym . . . gym . . . gym . . .

MRS. LYKE: Anybody?

CHILDREN: Gymnasium!

ELAINE: Gymnasium.

MRS. LYKE: What's the plural?

ELAINE: Add *s*. Gymnasiums.

MRS. LYKE: Right. Wendy?

WENDY: Bac . . . bacter . . . bacterium. Bacteriums.

MRS. LYKE: No, there's no such word. William?

WILLIAM: Add *ia*.

MRS. LYKE: Bacterium-ia?

WILLIAM: No, bacter*ia*.

MRS. LYKE: Right. Remember that. Sandy?

ROBERT: Mrs. Lyke, why is bacterium bacter*ia*, and gymnasium gymnasium*s*?

MRS. LYKE: Does anyone know? Well, I don't either. That's just the way we spell them and you have to remember them. Some spellings don't seem to make much sense, so just remember them. Tommy?

Although Mrs. Lyke provides pupils with immediate reinforcement (the correct spellings), in terms of what is known about learning, this whole approach to instruction is weak: there is unnecessary confusion, the development of set is to avoid finding patterns and to avoid generalizations, plus criticism of children's intelligent efforts. Moreover, words are inappropriately juxtaposed (*s* and *es* with *iums* and *ia*). And worst of all, meanings are completely ignored.

Mrs. Lyke's final comment makes some sense, but she drops the matter before children have a chance to grasp this aspect of the seeming arbitrariness of language.

16.

Miss Dale is trying to help her "linguistically impoverished" first-graders learn to express themselves orally in subject-verb-object sequence and to establish relationships between objects. While the rest of the class works on an assignment, Miss Dale displays to three of her pupils, Danny, Ada, and Tommy, sets of two large cards, on each of which is pictured an object with its label: a picture of a bird bearing the word *bird;* a picture of a tree bearing the word *tree,* etc. She holds up two cards. On one, a bird; on the other, a tree.

MISS DALE: Tell us about these, Danny.

DANNY: Bird. Tree.

MISS DALE: Can you put the bird in the tree?

DANNY: Bird.

MISS DALE: Listen to me, Danny. The bird is in the tree. The *bird* is *in* the *tree.* Can you say that?

DANNY: Bird inna tree.

MISS DALE: Listen carefully. The *bird* is *in* the *tree.*

DANNY: The bird inna tree.

MISS DALE: The bird - is - in - the - tree.

DANNY: The bird is - in - the - tree.

MISS DALE: Very good. Can you say that again?

DANNY: The bird is in the tree.

MISS DALE: Good! All together, children: The bird is in the tree.

CHILDREN AND TEACHER: The bird is in the tree.

MISS DALE: Very good, *very* good.
(Holds up pictures of *cat* and *house.*) Ada, can you put the cat in the house?

ADA: Cat in house.

TOMMY: Cat house, yuk! yuk!

MISS DALE: Listen: The - cat - is - in - the - house.

ADA: The cat in the house.

MISS DALE: Good! *The cat is in the house.*

ADA: The cat is in the house.

MISS DALE: Fine! Again.

ADA: The cat is in the house. The cat is in the house.

MISS DALE: Right! All together: The cat is in the house. (Holds up *horse* and *barn.*) Jacky?

When children do not use standard English, in particular when they do not discriminate parts of language that are visually distinctive in print, they need to develop these discriminations orally if they are to recognize the relevance of the printed symbols to the meaning they convey.

The repetition is appropriate.

Miss Dale takes care to make her words clearly distinctive and goes slowly enough so that the child can understand that what he thought was one word is really two. She also avoids reinforcing improper responses and immediately reinforces correct responses.

Miss Dale hints at meaning when she says, "Can you put the bird in the tree?" but Danny's solitary comment "Bird" suggests that while he hears her, he does not really understand. Miss Dale might well spend a bit of time making sure of meaning by actually "putting the bird in the tree." It is possible that none of the children might be grasping the signification of *in the.*

Finally note that Miss Dale ignores Tommy's irrelevant comment, thus helping to extinguish such responses.

17.

Miss Ryan often brings to her first-grade classroom large and colorful pictures of familiar animals, encourages the pupils to label the "parts," and then writes a little story using the labels and other descriptive words and phrases she has written on the chalkboard. Today she has brought a stuffed skunk, borrowed for the occasion from a community sporting goods store.

CHILDREN: What's that . . . a skunk?

HERBERT: Pew!

MISS RYAN: Pew? Why pew?

HERBERT: He stinks!

MISS RYAN: This one stinks?

HERBERT: He's dead! My brother says they stink.

MISS RYAN: Have you ever smelled one?

HERBERT: No, but they do! (More talk among the pupils.)

MISS RYAN: Who would like to tell me something about Mr. Skunk? Allan?

ALLAN: He has a big tail.

MISS RYAN: Would you mind if we said "bushy"?

ALLAN: No ma'am.

MISS RYAN: (Writing on board.) *Bushy tail.* (Points to tail.) Would you read this for us, Allan?

ALLAN: Bushy tail, bushy tail, bushy tail!

MISS RYAN: Fine. Someone else?

DEBORAH: He has little black eyes.

MISS RYAN: (Writes.) *Little black eyes.* Fine. Anyone else?

JACK: He has white on him, on his back.

MISS RYAN: (Running hand down back of animal.) What could we call this, this white . . .

BILLY: A stripe. A white stripe.

MISS RYAN: Is this all right with you, Jack? (Writes *white stripes down back.* Children offer other descriptive words and phrases which teacher writes in manuscript.) That's fine. Now you will need some other words and phrases for your stories. Here are some. (Writes on next section of blackboard several "helping" words and phrases which children will use to write their own expressions.)

eats insects and mice
sleeps in winter
fur makes coats
related to weasel family
North America

Miss Ryan begins with meaning and a concrete referent in order to help children broaden their "working" vocabulary and to help them learn to construct sentences. The use of pictures and models engages the attention of pupils at once.

No restrictions are placed on suggestions; pupils are free to suggest any descriptive words or phrases.

This is reading instruction based on pupils' writings, which adds a variety of concomitant learnings in a meaningful structure, thus making the learning stronger, more lasting, and transferable.

We object to Miss Ryan's substitution of *bushy* for *big*—at least in the manner she did. Why not accept Allan's adjective by saying, "Some people call it bushy, too. Can we say big and bushy?"

Miss Ryan does not lose sight of the originator of the descriptive words, but neither does she take away from Billy.

mammals
family dens
bad odor
pets
kills chickens
they . . .

ROBERT: Miss Ryan, what's this word? (Comes to board and points to *weasel*.)

MISS RYAN: *Weasel*. Here's what a weasel looks like (displays color picture). Does he look anything like a skunk?

ROBERT: No, he's littler.

MISS RYAN: Yes, he looks smaller. I'm not so sure he is, really. How about his fur?

ROBERT: It's littler, too.

MISS RYAN: Shorter fur? Yes, but they are in the same animal family—sort of brothers, maybe.

JACK: Like me and Jimmy?

MISS RYAN: Well, not quite. Let's read from the board: *The skunk has*. Together now.

CHILDREN: The skunk has . . .

MISS RYAN: *He has*

CHILDREN: He has . . .

MISS RYAN: Very good. *Eats insects and mice.*

CHILDREN: Eats insects and mice . . . (Teacher and children together read the description.)

MISS RYAN: Fine. Now who can read this for us? (Runs hand along phrase *sleeps in winter*.)

TOMMY: Sleeps in winter . . .

MISS RYAN: Fine! (Selects other descriptions which children read aloud.) Now let's write out stories. Perhaps we can make them into a big book to take to the sports store so Mr. Potter can show it to his customers. If you want to use a word not on the board, ask me.

MISS RYAN: Is anyone ready to read us his story? Jack?

JACK: They live in North America.
They are mammals.
Sometimes they kill chickens.
They live in a family den.
It has a fluffy tail.
They spray a bad odor.
They have black fur and white stipes (sic).
They make good pets.
They are related to weasals (sic).

> The move to a picture is valuable as supporting meaning because it adds another form and dimension of representation.

> Good follow-up activity as a motivating device.

> Pretty good for a January first-grader!

> This experience has struck some

people as quite "beyond first-graders," but it happened just as we record it. On the two pages following, you will find the September and January stories of two of the twelve pupils involved. They are typical productions.

18.

Mr. Keach often presents his fifth-grade pupils with "crazy sentences"—statements ambiguously expressed—that pupils then try to clarify by means of punctuation, or by shifting words and phrases to "make sense." This morning, noting that for some reason the children were restless, he interrupts their seat-work by writing on the board:

What do you think I will feed you for nothing and give you a drink.

JACK: Let me try! *What do you . . . What . . .* wait a minute! Let me think!

PUPILS: Let me!

MR. KEACH: Hold on! Who's next on the list? (A pupil refers to a wall chart titled *Assistant Teachers,* and calls out the name of the pupil in line for the position.)

MR. KEACH: O.K., Sandra. (Sandra joins Mr. Keach at his desk. Pupils immediately subside and many raise hands. Sandra calls "Tony!")

TONY: Well, *What do you think I will feed you for? Nothing? And give you a drink?* No, wait a minute!

SANDRA: You already said it. Try the punctuation! (Tony inserts the question marks.) All right, now what's the sense?

TONY: Well, it means he won't feed you for nothing and give you a drink!

SANDRA: Who agrees? (Most hands go up.)

LONNY: I got another way. Listen! *What do you think? I will feed you for nothing. And give you a drink.*

SANDRA: Punctuate it. (Lonny alters the sentence.) What's the sense?

LONNY: You get food and drink for nothing!

SANDRA: O.K., who agrees? (More hands.) Any more?

A nice blend of reading and "grammar" based on attention to meaning.

The use of ambiguous statements is an effective way to help pupils understand the role of punctuation in conveying meaning and to give them some insights into the nature of language. Here, pupils realize rather dramatically that punctuating is not simply a matter of applying rules, but is rather a matter of first getting meaning, and then using punctuation to communicate it.

The possibility of more than one meaning in the statement develops pupil set to look actively for meanings while reading.

This activity should make clear that punctuation is the graphic representation of the pitch, stress, and pause that enable us to communicate meanings orally. We would hope that at some point, Mr. Keach made this notion explicit if it did not come out in the discussions.

We like the "problems approach," which challenges pupils' abilities and then rewards them for their efforts.

The use of pupils as assistants provides leadership experience. Also, knowing that he will have his turn as assistant, the pupil is more likely to develop the set to look for alternatives, to ask ques-

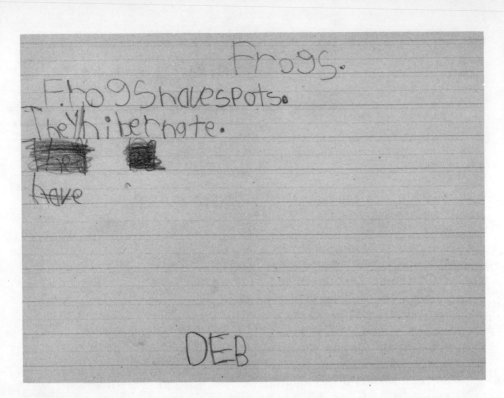

Frogs.

Frogs have spots.
They hibernate.
~~They~~ ~~have~~
have

DEB

Debbie

Racoons

They have whiskers.
They live in North America
Central America.
Racoons sleep in day.
He has little ears. They
They eat frogs, and turtles
fond fish. He has five
toes. They have black
masks.

104

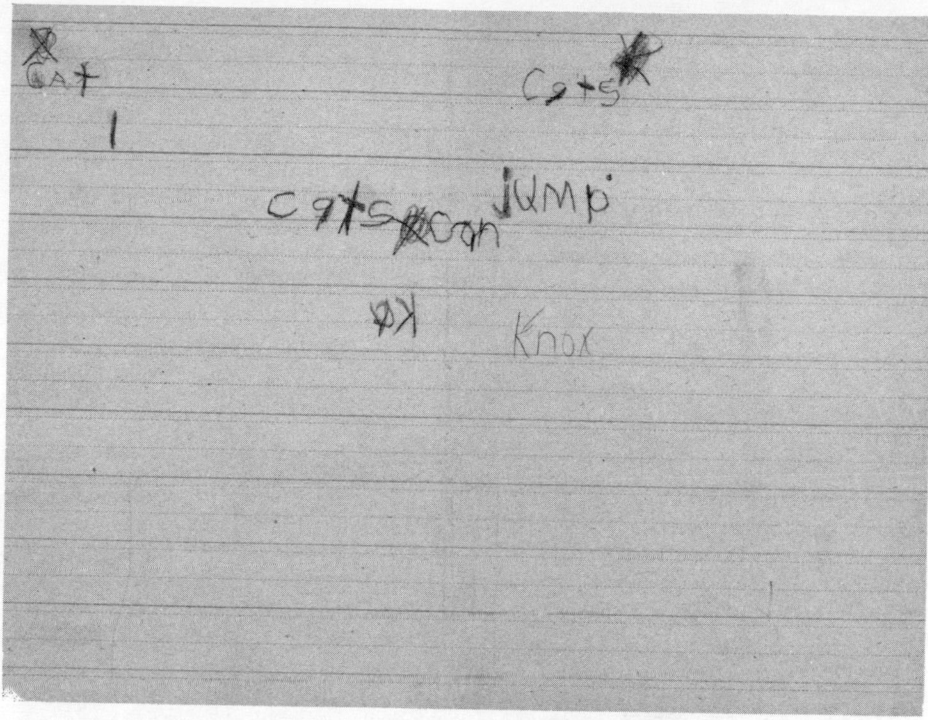

Cat   Cats

I

cats can   jump

K   Knox

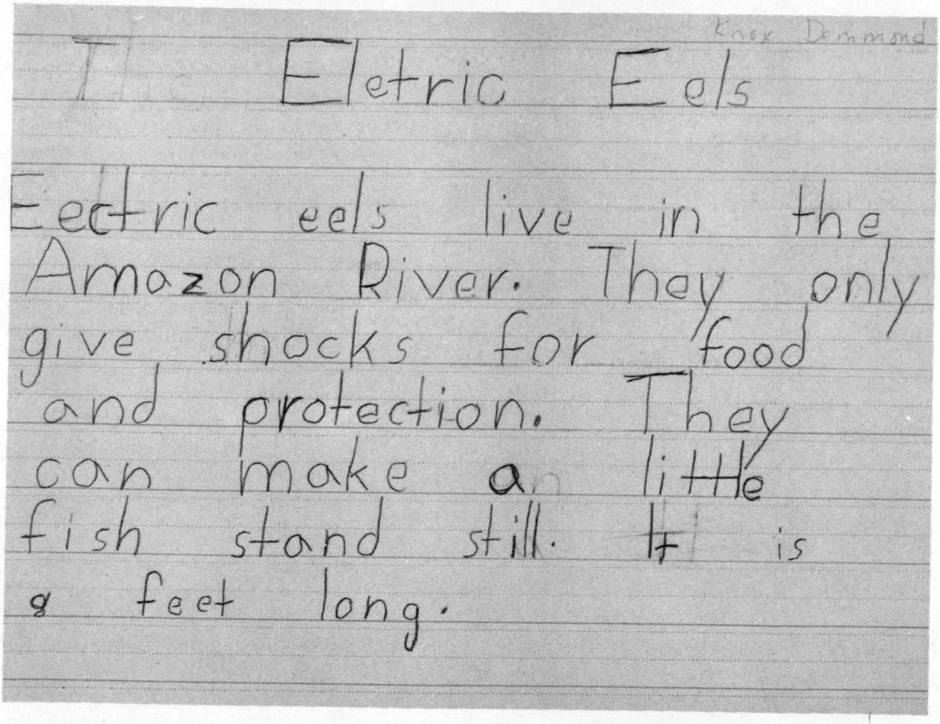

Knox Demmond

I   Eletric Eels

Eectric eels live in the
Amazon River. They only
give shocks for food
and protection. They
can make a little
fish stand still. It is
8 feet long.

ALBERT: Well, I think . . . well, if you stop with *What* . . . well, like *What! Do you think I will feed you for nothing and give you a drink?*

SANDRA: Try that, Albert. (Albert alters the sentence.)

Anyone disagree? (No hands.)

All right. (Starts for her seat.)

PUPILS: More, more!

MR. KEACH: Well, lots of you didn't have a chance to get to the board. Let's see what you can do with these crazy ones on paper. We can talk about them when you finish. (Writes on board).

Shall we eat grandmother?

Put the sweater on Bill.

For sale: Bicycle by a woman with a leather seat.

tions, and to figure out appropriate sequences. It should be remembered, however, that when only one pupil assists, some others may not be following the discussion. (This is the reason Mr. Keach asked that the last "batch" be done on paper.)

19.

Bruce, a fifth-grader in Mr. Bryan's room, is reading aloud to his classmates from a library book about animals.

BRUCE: 'Tom's favorite spot at the zoo was right in front of the lion's cage. He especially liked the father lion with his thick mane. In adjoining cages there were other members of the cat family: sleek tigers, leopards, cheetahs, and even the surly lynx, a cat almost without a tail.'

NED: Aw, how can a cat be a cat without no tail?

JOAN: My dog only has a little tail and he's a dog! He's a boxer!

NED: Yeah, but a cat's different. They got to have tails.

MR. BRYAN: O.K. *Almost.* Does that answer your question, Ned?

NED: Well, maybe.

MR. BRYAN: Go ahead and read, Bruce.

Mr. Bryan settled the issue rather neatly, but we think he missed an excellent opportunity not only to clarify children's concepts of *cat,* but also to introduce, at an appropriate moment, the whole notion of biological classification—its *whys* and its *hows.* To do so would add to children's vocabularies, provide information about the natural world and reveal how its living creatures are "ordered," show how man fits into the scheme of things, and ultimately perhaps lead to a discussion of the "races" of man and their distribution around the globe.

Thus Mr. Bryan might have intervened:

Mr. Bryan: O.K. *A'lmost.* Does that answer your question, Ned?

Ned: Well, maybe.

Mr. Bryan: You don't sound satisfied!

Ned: Well, lots of dogs have little tails, but I never saw a cat with a little tail, except this . . . this . . . lynx.

Mr. Bryan: I agree with you, but it seems the lynx is still a cat! I tell you what! Let's have a little detective game. Let's see if we can figure out why a cat is a cat, and not a cow or pig —or elephant! How about that?

Children: O.K.!

Ned: How do we do it?

Mr. Bryan: Well, what do you suggest? (Refuses to give out answers.)

Bert: Get a book of cats!

Mr. Bryan: Then what?

Bert: Look at them!

Mr. Bryan: Fine, but what for?

Ned: To see what cats look like!

Mr. Bryan might now arrange that pupils examine a variety of cats, including the domestic manx, to identify their characteristics, and then have pupils check the specific attributes of the lynx against these characteristics.

A next step would involve comparing several animals (dog, horse, snake, rat, monkey) by, say, having pupils list their particular characteristics, perhaps under such rubrics as "What they eat; what skin is like; how they move; what body is like; how they reproduce," and the like. Such comparisons would call forth various concepts used in classification, such as rodent, mammal, quadruped, carnivore (herbivore, omnivore), vertebrate, and the like.

Finally, the discussion could move to man himself, his unique qualities and his shared characteristics.

Mr. Bryan, as Mrs. Buck and Mr. Payne before him, might take a moment to suggest that cat is a label we give to a particular group of animals sharing common characteristics and habits. We could call them *flobs* if we wished!

20.

In Mrs. Rolf's fourth grade, Susan and Dan stand at the chalkboard listening intently to Mrs. Rolf as she reads aloud sentences from a list she has drawn up. The rest of the class, also listening intently, sit at their desks pencils poised. Tom stands at one end of the chalkboard with a copy of Mrs. Rolf's list. He is the first "Mr. Punctuation."

Mrs. Rolf reads in the manner of a recitation, emphasizing rather dramatically the pauses, pitches, and stresses suggested by the punctuation:

Mother called (pause) Jack (raised pitch, pause) what are (heavy stress) you doing (falling pitch and pause) eating again (rising pitch).

Susan and Dan turn to the board and as Mrs. Rolf repeats the sentence, rapidly sketch the punctuation marks they think her voice suggests. The seated pupils do the same. Tom surveys the board work and finds:

SUSAN: ,   ,   ——   ,   !
DAN: !   ——   ?   ?

Tom then reads the complete sentence from his list, observing as best he can Mrs. Rolf's intonations. He then turns to the class and calls on Billy, who goes to the board and alters Susan's work to:

,   !   ——   ,   ?

Tom then rereads the sentence and asks the class for their judgment. The pupils support Billy's interpretation. Tom then surveys Dan's work and repeats the procedure, calling on Ralph to correct Dan's interpretation. Tom then writes the sentence on the board.

Ralph now takes Tom's place, calls on two classmates to go to the board, and again all listen as Mrs. Rolf recites another sentence.

Mrs. Rolf, like Mr. Keach, wants her pupils to seek the reasons for things (in this activity—punctuation) rather than to try to solve problems by the mechanical application of rules.

Since she is not using ambiguous statements, however, her approach is the "reverse" of that taken by Mr. Keach. That is, instead of beginning with the written word, she presents the "problem" orally and asks that it be solved graphically. Both approaches are useful as ways of emphasizing the primacy of meaning in reading. Mrs. Rolf and Mr. Keach might well utilize both techniques to get at the same idea in different ways.

As do other teachers we have observed, Mrs. Rolf gives her pupils leadership experiences. In this connection, we suggest that she "turn loose" even more, permitting pupils to conduct the entire activity: select sentences, read them aloud, call on classmates, and evaluate results.

A possible weakness of this procedure is that most of the pupils may be inactive, with a favored few participating. Mrs. Rolf has the problem of "keeping everyone on his toes." How would you do it?

21.

Miss Dean's first-graders are gathered around her as, flow-pen in hand, she sits at her "easel chart."

MISS DEAN: Who would like to begin?

LISA: A big bear!

JACK: No, no! A bear. Not a big bear!

LISA: A bear.

CHILDREN: Big! Fat! Brown!

MISS DEAN: We'll have to start all over. Lisa.

LISA: A bear. Jack. (Miss Dean prints *A bear* at the top of the chart, and writes on successive lines whatever word the children suggest.)

JACK: A *fat* bear. Jane.

JANE: A fat *brown* bear. Joe.

JOE: A fat brown . . . *funny* bear! Bill.

BILL: A fat brown funny bear *fell down*. Connie.

MISS DEAN: Hold on! Let me catch up. All right, Connie.

CONNIE: A fat, brown, funny bear fell down *in the river.*

MISS DEAN: Fine! Now let's put it all together. Yvonne, you read these words—we call them *adjectives*, because they tell something about our bear. Yvonne? (Yvonne reads and Miss Dean writes: A - fat - brown - funny - bear - fell - down - in - the - river.) Very good. Who would like to read the whole sentence? (Alice reads.) Fine, Alice.

CHILDREN: Again, again! A dog! An elephant! A fat pig!

Miss Dean's pupils are *reading* because the words they dictate are words they know, having experienced them in one way or another. Hence they are able to "take meaning to, in order to get meaning from . . . !"

Moreover, the pupils are learning not only how sentences "grow" and how to build them, but also how to create (and we hope appreciate) details that give life and color to efforts to portray "what is."

Permitting pupils to call on their classmates gives them the experience of conducting their own activity, and frees Miss Dean to attend to the task of printing what is said.

As for the reference to *adjectives*, we cannot object so long as Miss Dean does not permit matters of terminology to become obtrusive, or to think, as did Mrs. Cope, that the ability to call a word signifies understanding.

This kind of activity is an excellent "lead in" to language in print, for it helps pupils realize that reading represents the spoken word, gives them a meaningful stock of words known in print, and gets them accustomed to the formality of written language.

22.

Mrs. Coles teaches the second grade. Her room, of conventional size, harbors 31 pupils. From the ceiling hang decorations and mobiles created by her pupils. Under the windows are low bookcases filled with all sorts of trade books, 40 or 50 of them, some purchased by Mrs. Coles, some brought by pupils, others borrowed from the school and community libraries.

On the bookcases are, in random array, several flowerpots; a terrarium sporting a variety

Mrs. Coles obviously believes that:

a. One learns to read by reading what interests him most.

b. Since interests differ, materials ought to differ.

c. It is better to lure children into reading than to subject them to formal "lessons."

of insects, a frog, and a small turtle; two large folio editions of colored reproductions of paintings by Van Gogh and Utrillo; a small display of papier-mâché dragons created by class members; a box of tone flutes; a small xylophone; and an autoharp.

One of two small tables in the two "rear" corners of the room is littered with magazines: *Life, Holiday, National Geographic, Arizona Highways,* and two or three children's magazines. On the other are hard-cover editions of books on animal life: birds, insects, reptiles, and the like. A rocking chair is nearby.

On a larger table between these two is a tape recorder fitted with a device for plugging in eight headsets. Other audio-visual devices are stored under the table (there is no storage closet): a record player, filmstrip and overhead projectors, together with an assortment of discs (musical and narrative), filmstrips for learning and for fun, and language tapes recorded by both teacher and pupils.

All sorts of charts and bulletins line the available wall space: *In Africa We Would See* (list of animals); *To Make Flour Paste* (directions for mixing flour, salt, and water); *Who Reads This Week?* (names of pupils slated to read to class each day before dismissal); *Words We Like* (collected, printed out, and reviewed daily by two "Word Hunters"); *Story of the Week* (chosen on Fridays from those read by pupils).

Today, Mrs. Coles quiets the "before school" hubbub by asking, "Who would like to read the schedule?"

Jane comes forward and reads: "Story books—Numbers—Language—Science—Projects." (Pupils have been working in small groups making an illustrated dictionary to present to their first-grade friends down the hall.) Mrs. Coles thanks Jane and then asks the class, "Now what will you be doing when you have any time on your hands?"

Pupils call out, "Read . . . go to the bathroom . . . play number game . . . play *sounds* game . . . work on aquarium . . . practice on tone flutes . . . review spelling."

Mrs. Coles stops. "Very good. This is quite a list! If you go to practice your music, be sure to shut the door, won't you?

"Who would like to read this for us?" Allan

d. Consciousness of learning something is an educational disaster; hence, the less "schooly" a schoolroom is, the better it is for learning.

e. What children learn should somehow relate to the world in which they live (or should live!): the world of art, of music, of nature, of people.

f. Reading is meaningful to the extent that it is useful.

g. Growth in reading ability does not depend altogether (or even largely) on the use of "readers."

h. Children learn to manage themselves by having the *chance* to manage themselves.

i. The best way to help a child in trouble is to pay attention to that child.

j. Molehills (Alton and Ned) are not mountains.

There would be an advantage in having paintings representing styles different from those of the two French artists.

We would have liked to be in Mrs. Coles' class.

comes forward and does so. He is unable to say "practice." Mrs. Coles pronounces it for him and, later, writes the word under his name in a notebook containing the reading record of each child.

"All right, fine. Now we can go on with our plans.

"I have a new story at the listening table, and I'd especially like for these people to hear it." (Calls out eight names.) Her tape presents a humorous story showing the importance of, and some tips for, correct spelling. "When you've heard it, I will give Tony some question cards so you can play your team game." This consists of seeing which group of four can answer the most questions asked—and later answered—by the taped voice. The eight pupils go to their listening stations. Dick handles the machine.

"Elsie and Mabel, on my desk is a new set of word cards. Will you try them out for me? Mark the ones you think we need to put on the chart. You can use the next room where it's quiet. Now, a few of you can come to the rocker with me if you are having any storybook troubles." Mrs. Coles takes three new books from her desk and goes to the rocking chair. Four pupils join her, books in hand, while the rest take from their desks books they have chosen, or go to the bookcase to find new ones.

Two boys begin to wander about, silently peering over shoulders and simulating listening to the tape. Mrs. Coles says, "Alton and Ned, look here." She holds up a new Dr. Seuss book. The boys go to her and take the book. "Can we read it together?" They disappear behind the flower planter. Mrs. Coles turns to her little group.

"While Ellen and I talk a bit, you three may look at this I brought from home." (A new issue in a popular series.) The children receive it eagerly. Mrs. Coles takes Ellen on her knee, saying, "Ellen, read me some of your story . . ."

After listening for several minutes, Mrs. Coles interrupts to say, "Ellen, I think we can help. Let me get our chart." As she gets up, there is a sudden burst of laughter from Alton and Ned, who run to her waving the Dr. Seuss book. Mrs. Coles quietly arranges that they practice certain passages and read them to the class as soon as she finishes with her group. The two boys return to their places, giggling and exhibiting their book to classmates as they go.

Mrs. Coles returns with the chart, and with a notebook in which she will later jot down information gained from Ellen's oral reading. She then addresses the other three children: "We need your help with these kinds of words." She writes on the chart in a group:

church
chicken
chimney
choke
chain

and in a second group:

place
plum
play
please

"What do you notice about this group of words? . . . Very good. Ellen, will you try them? Excellent, except for this one. Good! Good girl! Now how about this group . . . ?"

23.

Billy, a third-grader in Mr. Jack's room, is sitting alone at a tape recorder in the cloakroom, dictating what he saw and did on the way to school this morning. The rest of the pupils are studying a series of scrambled comic-strip frames featuring *Peanuts,* which Mr. Jack has projected on a screen via an opaque projector. Each frame is numbered, and pupils are arranging on their papers what they think is the appropriate sequence—one that "tells the story."

After a bit, Billy appears with the recorder, which he puts by Mr. Jack's desk. He then joins his classmates in the Peanuts game. When all have finished, Mr. Jack snaps off the projector and gives the scrambled frames to Mitchell and Dave who go into the cloakroom to arrange them in the sequence they recorded.

Mr. Jack then turns on Billy's recording:

Well, first thing was I seen the milkman an' I seen . . . uh . . . milkman an' Buddy he come out an' he . . . an' he . . . uh . . .

To help his "verbally impoverished" pupils learn to express themselves more clearly, Mr. Jack uses the tape recorder to enable individuals, with help, to analyze their monologs. In this way, thoughts are reconstructed in the direction of "Standard English" found in texts and trade books.

A series of pupil reading actions open to teacher reinforcement take place fairly rapidly.

Letting Billy handle the tape recorder makes him a "party" to the affair rather than an outsider being criticized.

Having pupils read aloud the corrected monolog provides practice in saying and hearing clear expression.

The projection of the *Peanuts* frames is an engaging way to gives me some of his Cheerios an' him and me seen some guys . . . uh . . . well, they was chalkin' on the walk an' Buddy hollers out . . . uh . . .

Mr. Jack turns the recorder off, saying, "That's good, Billy. This gives us something to work with just fine. Thanks. Now help me replay this, but remember to cut fast when I tell you." He rewinds the tape and turns to the chalkboard. "O.K., let's go."

Billy turns the recorder on, and all listen. When Mr. Jack signals, Billy stops the tape, and Mr. Jack writes rapidly what he and the pupils heard. This continues until Billy's recording is transcribed in full.

"All right," Mr. Jack says, "we'll write our suggestions over here. O.K., Billy, go ahead."

Billy frowns. "Just cut the *Well* first, then . . . uh . . . say, 'The first thing was I *saw* the milkman.' "

"Good, any comments?" Billy makes the correction. Loren speaks up, "Cut the *was*. It don't go."

Mr. Jack looks questioningly at the class. Pupils nod "yes." He then looks at Billy, who erases the *was*, but immediately gets a chorus of "You got to put it back in after *saw* or it don't make sense!"

Billy adds *was* and reads the revision, "The first thing I saw was the milkman."

"Sounds great! Try it again."

"The first thing I saw was the milkman."

"Together, everybody, *loud!*"

"The first thing I saw was the milkman!"

"Again! Come on!"

The children repeat, loudly.

"Great going! Jane, you try it. (Jane does.) Sammy, you try it. (Sammy does.) Tony? Randall?" One child after another gets his chance to repeat the sentence. Finally, "All right, good. Now, Bill?"

"Well, uh, cut out all that up to Buddy. Say, 'And Buddy come . . . came out and . . .' " A child interrupts:

"Come . . . came out of where?"

"Out of the house!"

"Then write it in!"

"Billy, now read your whole story, then we'll read it with you."

" 'The first thing I saw was the milkman. Then Buddy came out of his house and gave

help pupils learn to "reason through" the sequence of events in a story.

Note that by letting Billy have the first crack at self-correction, the threat otherwise implicit in this technique is drastically reduced, though probably not eliminated.

Finally, but not least, Mr. Jack provides his unwitting pupils with an interesting "reading lesson" by way of the language-experience approach.

me some of his Cheerios. He and I saw some guys chalking on the walk, so Buddy hollers out . . .' "

"Good! Now let's all read it, with some muscle, but not too much muscle!"

" 'The first thing I saw . . .' "

"All right, now. No, we don't have time for another right now, but Billy, you can take the recorder back and feed in another story if you want to. We'll have some time this afternoon. Who comes after Billy? Fine. Now, how about Mr. Peanuts? Dave, you and Mitchell read off your number sequence. Check your papers, everybody. In a minute, Dave can project the frames in the order they call them, and we'll check up on them, O.K.?"

24.

Mrs. Welch discloses the following episode written on chart paper for her second-graders:

Pam made some chocolate candy.
She took it to the front yard to sell to neighbors.
She made a big sign that read:
BUY MY CANDY. GEORGE SAYS IT IS GOOD.

MRS. WELCH: Read my story to yourselves. All right, would you read it for us, Elaine? (Elaine obliges, tripping on *chocolate* and *neighbors* and having to be helped by classmates.)

ELAINE: It makes me hungry!

MRS. WELCH: Do you think the candy is good?

CHILDREN: Yes, yes!

MRS. WELCH: Why do you think so?

ELAINE: Well, Pam made it.

MRS. WELCH: Who is Pam?

TOMMY: Well, she's a girl.

MRS. WELCH: Yes. Does that mean the candy is good?

NANCY: I don't know any Pam. Who's Pam?

MRS. WELCH: Do you have to know a Pam?

SANDY: Who's George?

CHILDREN: Yes, who's George?

MRS. WELCH: What about George?

CHILDREN: George—he says the candy is good!

MRS. WELCH: So?

The notion of critical analysis can be presented early in the course of reading.

Having Elaine read aloud is one way to give rather immediate knowledge of results to those students who do try to read it themselves.

Mrs. Welch's questioning technique subtly pushes pupils to a conclusion about Pam's "sponsor." Note that she does this without rejecting a single pupil remark.

However, we suggest that she might have responded to Sandy's last remark with something like, "Why would you think it's good?" (We are not suggesting that children be taught to trust *no* one; just that Mrs. Welch be consistent!)

Would you say that Mrs. Welch is using the "problems approach" in this episode? She does make some progress toward getting pupils to be less gullible, but doesn't really quite make it. It is unlikely that she could "make it" with many children of this age who do not customarily engage in imag-

NELSON: Aw, who's old George!

MRS. WELCH: Yes, who's old George! He says Pam's candy is good.

ALICE: I don't know any George.

MRS. WELCH: Isn't it enough that George says the candy is good?

CHILDREN: No, no!

MRS. WELCH: Why not?

CHILDREN: We don't know any George.

MRS. WELCH: What difference does that make? Are you saying that you don't believe George? Well, whose name should Pam use if she wants to sell her candy—if she wants people to know the candy is good?

SANDY: Put in *Mother* says its good!

MRS. WELCH: Why mother?

SANDY: Well, mother knows if it's good!

MRS. WELCH: You can believe what mother says?

CHILDREN: Yes, yes!

MRS. WELCH: And you can't believe what George says . . . ?

DANNY: Well, you just don't believe any old body—any old George-Porge!

MRS. WELCH: What's the best way to find out whether Pam's candy is good?

CHILDREN: Eat it, eat it!

MRS. WELCH: Well, that makes sense. Suppose Pam put "MRS. WELCH SAYS ITS GOOD." How about that?

SANDY: Well, we would know it's good, then.

MRS. WELCH: How about eating it . . .

ining a sequence of abstract operations. Yet Mrs. Welch is to be commended for pushing them in this direction. Until this kind of reasoning is in hand, reading is perforce very limited.

Note that successful or not, this effort focuses attention on the elements in the passage that determine its meaning.

25.

Mr. Beal's sixth-grade pupils have just put the finishing touches on their folders of "Colonial Life" and are busy creating colorful covers.

A visitor, Tom Engle's father, enters and is greeted warmly by Mr. Beal, who then turns to Tom.

MR. BEAL: Tom, introduce your father.

TOM: This is my father.

MR. BEAL: Glad you came in. Like to hear what we're doing? (Visitor nods and sits at desk. Children visibly aware of the presence of a stranger; they sit straight, eyes to the front.)

Mr. Beal's method and technique speak for themselves. His aim is worthy; his procedure disastrous. Observe what we may term the "catalog of evils":

a. The "model" behavior of the pupils at the appearance of Tom's father suggests that they have been threatened with reprisals if they "cut up" in front of visitors.

b. His nagging of Cathy reveals

We have just finished our reports on colonial life in America . . .

MILTON: In the United States! You said . . .

MR. BEAL: Yes, yes, I know. How about raising your hand?

MILTON: You said . . .

MR. BEAL: All right, all right. You don't just holler out when you feel like it. Now relax! Show our guest that we have manners.

Jane, you had the best one on our last topic of why the colonists broke with England. Read it for Mr. Engle. (Jane demurs.) Don't you want to show how well you write? O.K., then. How about Cathy? Well, let's stand up straight and look this way!

CATHY: 'As time went on, the colonists became more and more angry at the way the British were treating them . . .'

MR. BEAL: That's wrong. You should say, *'Many of the colonists.'* Go on.

CATHY: 'Many of the colonists . . . and they were . . .'

MR. BEAL: Well, start over and read the complete thought!

CATHY: 'As time went on, the colonists—I mean —*many* of the colonists became more and more angry at the way the British were treating them. They were especially angry at being taxed without representation . . .'

MR. BEAL: Meaning what?

CATHY: I got that from the encyclopedia.

MR. BEAL: Sure, but what does it mean?

CATHY: What does what mean?

MR. BEAL: Taxed without representation!

CATHY: Well, it means being taxed without representation.

MR. BEAL: Well of course! That's what you just said! What does it *mean*? What is taxation without representation?

CATHY: (Floundering.) It costs money.

MR. BEAL: What costs money? Everything costs money. What about taxes? What is a tax?

CATHY: Income tax?

MR. BEAL: There wasn't any income tax then. What do you do when you pay taxes? Your father pays your taxes. What does he do? What did the colonists do? *Think!*

CATHY: (In desperation.) Sales tax? No representation . . . I don't know!

MR. BEAL: All right, all right! This isn't funny, you know. Tomorrow I'm getting each one of

what appears to be sadism, brought out by the presence of a "third party." The fact that his questioning brings out no clue to the answer suggests that he prefers the inquisition to Cathy's learning.

c. Mr. Beal's refusal to accept Milton's correction makes it clear to pupils that he is more concerned with image than with the truth of things.

d. We are not sure that suggesting alternative procedures would save Mr. Beal. Are you?

you up here and we'll see how funny it is. (To the visitor: You see what we go through most of the time.) We sure are on the ball today, of all days, too! I'm sure Mr. Engle is impressed. All right, get out your arithmetic books, and no noise, and fast! Let's see if we can do some better with *that*.

26.

In her first grade, from the beginning of school, Miss Tyson takes time each day to play language games with her pupils. For this purpose, she has collected a number of three-dimensional objects: a rag doll, three or four clay animals, some articles of clothing, several kinds of artificial flowers, some toy cars and trucks, and so on. Today the children have gathered on the floor around Miss Tyson, who is holding up a small, red fire truck. The following exchange is carried on quite rapidly.

MISS TYSON: This is a truck.
CHILDREN (in unison): This is a truck.
MISS TYSON: This is a truck.
CHILDREN: This is a truck.
MISS TYSON: This is a red truck.
CHILDREN: This is a red truck.
MISS TYSON: This is a red truck.
CHILDREN: This is a red truck.
MISS TYSON: This is a fire truck.
CHILDREN: This is a fire truck.
MISS TYSON: This is a red fire truck.
CHILDREN: This is a red fire truck.
MISS TYSON: Is this a red truck?
CHILDREN: Yes, this is a red truck.
MISS TYSON: Is the fire truck red?
CHILDREN: Yes, the fire truck is red.
MISS TYSON: What is this?
CHILDREN: This is a red fire truck.
MISS TYSON: This is a red fire truck.
CHILDREN: This is a red fire truck.
MISS TYSON: Here is a cat.
CHILDREN: Here is a cat.
MISS TYSON: Where is the cat?
CHILDREN: Here is the cat.
MISS TYSON: Here is a fat cat.
CHILDREN: Here is a fat cat.
MISS TYSON: Where is the fat cat?

This kind of activity can be a very useful device for expanding children's meaningful vocabulary. Their expressive abilities, their feeling for the sequence and rhythm of the language, and perhaps above all, their habits of precision in both usage and pronunciation—all obviously relevant to reading.

However, in a mass group many children will not be responding properly, and the teacher will not be able to spot them. Thus this procedure may well reinforce erroneous usage and pronunciation.

One solution is to employ this procedure with groups of, say, five where the variant responses can be spotted and corrected immediately, e.g., divide the class into such groups and have each group or at least several of them respond together in turn. These individuals can be identified. However some of the motivational advantages of unison responding would be lost.

CHILDREN: Here is the fat cat.
MISS TYSON: Is the cat fat?
CHILDREN: Yes, the cat is fat.
MISS TYSON: Here is a shoe . . .

27.

Mr. Hodgson has asked Jack Brown, one of his seventh-graders, to copy on the chalkboard a "table" and list of words sketched out on paper. After a few moments, Jack produces the following:

Mr. Hodgson is trying to get his pupils to see that while words (as concepts) often appear simple, they are usually deceptively complex. Discussions such as this

HARMFUL	HELPFUL	BOTH	DOESN'T FIT	WORDS
				knife
				bacteria
				war
				ice cream
				pain
				red
				Jack Brown
				speeding
				exams
				words
				baseball
				tree

MR. HODGSON: O.K. See what you can do with these. Let's do it in three minutes this time. Begin! (Pupils write. When time is called, Jack goes to the board and leads the discussion.)

JACK: All right. Let's start with my name. Sam?

SAM: Put it under number one! (Laughter.) Naw, number three, Both.

JACK: Why?

SAM: Well, you could help me with my homework. Or you might sock me on the nose. Better not try, though!

JACK: O.K. Any comments? All right. (Writes his name in column three.) Now how about *knife?* Lucy?

LUCY: Under number three, too. It can cut you or it can cut a piece of cheese.

JACK: Any comments? (Writes *knife* under Both.) How about *bacteria?* Jim?

can help children realize that the world is not "black and white," but various shades of gray—that people, things, concepts, and human activities are complicated, so that solutions to problems are rarely simple solutions.

These pupils are being helped to "go beyond translation" to analyze, evaluate, predict, draw inferences, and the like.

As pupils become more sophisticated in their understanding of the interrelationships among concepts, the level of difficulty (complexity) can be raised to include such concepts as love, obedience, justice, and democracy.

Mr. Hodgson obviously believes that pupils can and should con-

JIM: Under *Harmful.*
(Several hands go up.)
JACK: All right. Tony?
TONY: Well, Mrs. Chilson said there are good germs—bacteria—too. Like the ones that sour milk so we can have buttermilk . . .
JACK: O.K.?
PUPILS: Yes—under Both!
JACK: All right!
MR. HODGSON: Good, Tony! Now just for kicks, how about bacteria in the human system—our bodies? (Silence.) Nobody knows? Well, let's find out. Who wants to find out and report tomorrow? Coleen? O.K. You may have first spot in the morning, Coleen. Very good!
JACK: How about *war?* Cindy?
CINDY: Harmful. Put under number one.
(Several pupils call out "No, number three—Both!")
JACK: Wait a minute, wait a minute!
TOM: Wars aren't helpful.
ALICE: Some wars are, like . . . like the first and second World Wars! They saved democracy!
TOM: Sure, and look at all the people that got killed. Was *that* helpful?
MABEL: Well, suppose we had lost . . .
After nearly a whole class period of discussion (some perfunctory, some heated), pupils finish with the chart:

duct as many of their own activities as they can manage.

HARMFUL	HELPFUL	BOTH	DOESN'T FIT
war	baseball	knife	red
	exams	bacteria	tree
		ice cream	
		pain	
		Jack Brown	
		speeding	
		words	

CHAPTER VII

EPILOGUE

We have come to the end of our book. To be consistent, we should now summarize our summaries for you. But we feel that to do so would be redundant, preachy, and boring. And if there's anything reading should *not* be, it's redundant, preachy, and boring.

Of course we could resort to exhortation. We could plead with you to never, never, *never* forget the heart and soul of learning to read: children must enjoy what they read; they enjoy only what is meaningful; they have to take meanings *to* language in print; and the only meanings they can take are those that arise from their own experiences.

We could urge you to give children of all ages the freedom to talk about things and people and ideas—to "play with" language in order to sharpen their powers of expression and help them understand the tricks oral and written language can play, especially the trick of word-magic.

We could press you to remember that it is not what you do that matters in the end; it is what children do. And it is the child's set that determines what he attends to and does. So you have to work at developing that set to get him self-energized in the right direction.

We could go on and entreat you never to associate learning with threat, or to punish mistakes, or to pit child against child in unequal competition for praise, special privileges, and gold stars. Rather, strive to arrange meaningful activities that every child will find rewarding.

And finally, we could suggest that you adapt some of our vignettes and try them in your classroom. From there, you can go on to develop more exciting ways of your own to help children read for meaning.

But we really do not believe in exhortation. If our book has meaning for you, you will act on the notions we have suggested. If not, well, we've enjoyed our visit with you. Good luck and better teaching, even if you won't listen to reason!

INDEX